Amongst Barbarians

A Play

Michael Wall

FOR PRODUCTION ENQUIRIES

UNITED STATES AND CANADA
Info@SamuelFrench.com
1-866-598-8449

UNITED KINGDOM AND EUROPE
Theatre@SamuelFrench-London.co.uk
020-7255-4302

Each title is subject to availability from Samuel French, depending upon country of performance. Please be aware that *AMONGST BARBARIANS* may not be licensed by Samuel French in your territory. Professional and amateur producers should contact the nearest Samuel French office or licensing partner to verify availability.

MUSIC USE NOTE

IMPORTANT BILLING AND CREDIT REQUIREMENTS

AMONGST BARBARIANS

First staged at the Royal Exchange Theatre, Manchester, on 9th February, 1989. The cast was as follows:

Bryan	Dominic Keating
Ralph	Ronan Vibert
Gaolers	Tariq Yunus
	Zubie Dar
	Anji Dar
Lawyer	Sakuntala Ramanee
George	Christopher Hancock
Wendy	Avril Elgar
Lilly	Kathy Burke
Toni	Rosalind March
Barman	Ricardo Sibelo

Directed by **James Maxwell**
Designed by **David Millard**
Lighting by **Vincent Herbert**
Sound by **Alastair Goolden**
Fights Director **Nicholas Hall**

CHARACTERS

Bryan, from north London, aged 20
Ralph, English, but has a slightly Americanized accent;
    early 20s, possibly late 20s
Gaoler, large, tough Sikh man, good English
Lawyer, elegant Tamil woman, excellent English, 30s
George, Bryan's father, north Londoner with bad nerves,
    40s
Wendy, Bryan's mother, loud, early 40s
Lilly, Bryan's sister, heavy, young mother, aged 17-19
Toni, Ralph's mother, glamorous, 40, perhaps older
Barman, Malay or Chinese, attractive to the women,
    young

Set in Penang, Malaysia; in two hotel bedrooms, a bar, and
a prison cell

Time—the late Eighties

ACT I

SCENE 1

Prison cell in Penang, Malaysia. It should be brightly-lit and spacious—white walls, hot

If possible, signs of life behind the cell, where other prisoners occupy a sort of open area

Bryan and Ralph have come in. They are dejected, exhausted. Bryan is twenty, Ralph is older

Ralph slumps on his bed. He has a Walkman. Bryan seems lost. He presents an incongruous sight here, and indeed he has little idea of where he is or what's happened to him. Silence for a while

Bryan Well, that's us nicely bolloxed, ennit?

Ralph says nothing

Very nicely bolloxed. Thank you very much. Oi—I'm talking to you.
Ralph Yeah.
Bryan Oh, you can hear me; I thought you couldn't hear. I thought perhaps you had that wonderful instrument you call brain switched off.
Ralph I can hear you.
Bryan Well, that's something. That fucking persecutor, he made it all up, didn't he? We never done half the things he said we done. Well, *I* never; I dunno what *you* done.
Ralph Prosecutor.
Bryan What?
Ralph It's prosecutor, not persecutor, although, I suppose... (*He stops*)
Bryan Bollocks.
Ralph Yeah, well, why don't you try and give things their proper names, you know?
Bryan I'll give you your proper name, pal.
Ralph All right.
Bryan All right. I mean, they took no notice about that copper, did they? The

one in charge, who—what's-'is-name—solicited, the one who solicited the twenty thousand dollars. That's a fucking bribe he was trying to get—I dunno what else you'd call it. They failed to take that into account.

Ralph They did.

Bryan What?

Ralph They did take it into account.

Bryan What?

Ralph What d'you mean "what"?

Bryan When?

Ralph It's a separate issue. It's got nothing to do with our guilt or innocence.

Bryan 'Course it's got to do with it!

Ralph All right...

Bryan 'Course it has. Copper takes a bribe, it weakens the whole case, dunnit? Stands to reason. The whole case against us is rendered suspect.

Ralph We're guilty as charged, man.

Bryan Yeah, I ain't saying—I'm just saying, when the Court of Law is dealing with scumbags like him, they can't be relied upon, quite frankly. I mean, an English court would have slung it out, wouldn't they? There ain't nothing dodgier than a bent copper.

Ralph Yeah.

Bryan 'Course I ain't saying I'm *innocent*—I just ain't as guilty as you, that's all.

Ralph What difference does it make?

Bryan That fucking lawyer, she said she'd look for loopholes and that—what was that if it weren't a loophole? Bent coppers supplying the information. In England they'd've chucked it out and we'd be down the boozer now.

Ralph I doubt it.

Bryan 'Course we fucking would. Bent copper, there's no case.

Ralph It's not "bent"; they take it for granted everyone's working a scam...

Bryan Yeah, but that ain't——

Ralph The Customs found us with it in our fucking Y-fronts, man—now smarten up.

Bryan I know they did; I ain't contesting that. That ain't contested. But what I'm saying is—who tipped 'em off? Number one cunt.

Ralph All right.

Bryan I mean, don't try to tell me they're gonna hang us on that 'cos it just don't stand up. For fuck's sake, how can it? I mean, fair's fair, ennit? It's not as though we fucking killed anybody, is it? I mean, who did we kill? It's just not realistic. It isn't a realistic sentence to pass. I mean, why not hanging for pinching a loaf of bread or poking your best mate's missis or something? It's prehistoric. I'll take what I got coming, but no way can you tell me hanging is appropriate for a thing like this. It's just not playing the fucking game. Oi—is it?

Ralph No, it's not a game.

Bryan That's what I'm saying. I couldn't believe it when that cunt read that out. Hanged by the neck until you are dead... Jesus. Who'd he think he's talking to? Fucking multiple murderer or something? Who'd I fucking kill? I hate killers; I think they should be hanged. But I ain't one. It doesn't describe me at all. I'm not even fucking twenty-one. They knew that, didn't they? I mean, that was pointed out to them, wasn't it? That I'm under-age?

Ralph Yeah.

Bryan Well, there ought to be a fucking law against it.

Ralph There is a law and you got on the wrong end of it.

Bryan You an' all. Don't try and tell me you ain't gonna get the same. That's the only satisfaction I've received so far.

Ralph Why don't you just shut up about the law. If the law's an ass you're the shit that comes out of it.

Bryan No, I'm saying an international law—there's got to be an international law, respected by all nations alike, which it's a crime to hang an under-aged person for this. Anyway, they can't hang a fucking Englishman.

Ralph Yeah, well, that's just what they can do.

Bryan What—foreigners hang an Englishman? Leave it out; it's a complete contradiction in terms. I mean, who gave 'em their fucking legal system in the first place...

Ralph Oh, man...

Bryan No, go on—who give it to 'em? We did. Fucking muggins as usual— we give 'em everything, then they go and turn on us.

Ralph You know, in certain circumstances I suppose you could be quite entertaining...

Bryan I'd been all right if it hadn't been for you. Why didn't you fucking leave me alone? Heroin? I never touched the stuff back home. I hate fucking pushers; they should all be shoved down the lavatory... What you laughing at now, you cunt? You're always laughing at something. You done that in court, I seen you. No wonder they was indisposed against us, what with you smirking like that all the bleedin' time...

Ralph Maybe I find the whole thing funny.

Bryan Oh, yeah, fucking hilarious. Got me in stitches here. I expect you'll be laughing when they put that rope round your neck an' all. Oh, I don't wanna think about it. Gives me the fucking creeps. And another thing: that fucking accent of yours. I could see they hated you the moment you opened your mouth. What you trying to be—Clint Eastwood or something? You an Englishman or not?

Ralph Yeah, I'm English.

Bryan Well, why don't you fucking talk like one?

Ralph I've done a lot of travelling, Bryan.

Bryan Well, I wish you fucking hadn't. I wish you'd stayed home and sat in front of the telly, instead of... Why the fuck couldn't you have left me alone? I was all right.

Ralph Oh, yeah!

Bryan I was.

Ralph Yeah, you were wonderful.

Bryan I ain't saying I was wonderful; I'm saying I was all right. I didn't need...

Ralph You needed the money! Well, you wanted it. Quit telling yourself lies, why don't you? You did it for the bread. Twenty-five thousand and a first-class flight on to Australia—you couldn't resist it. A fortnight in Oz, then back home like the fucking Sugar Plum Fairy—Look Ma! You're a victim of your own greed. The new English disease, or haven't you heard?

Bryan Bollocks...

Ralph ...That's why you were perfect. Or we *thought* you were perfect.

Bryan I wasn't perfect, was I?

Ralph You were not. You were a complete asshole.

Bryan You're lucky I haven't broken your fucking neck for you by now.

Ralph I am?

Bryan Fucking lucky. I tell you, they shouldn't've put us in the same cell together, 'cos I'm gonna do for you.

Ralph Yeah, well, I sleep with one eye open.

Bryan You fucking would.

Ralph Because that's the only way you'd do it, pal...

Bryan Stop calling me pal; I ain't your pal...

Ralph You're all talk, like all the English these days...

Bryan You don't half fucking know a lot about the English considering you don't live there no more...

Ralph ...They're gonna hang you by the neck until you're fucking dead and then you'll be number one jerk.

Bryan Yeah, well, they're gonna hang you too, mate, so you're not so bloody smart, are you?

Ralph You should've gone to Margate for your holidays.

Bryan I nearly did. You don't know how true you spoke—I nearly did! 'Cept I won this fucking trip in a raffle. (*He laughs*) Fucking laugh, ennit? That's your sort of humour, ennit? Cunt wins a foreign holiday in a raffle, ends up getting himself topped. You like all that, don't you?

Ralph (*seriously*) Yeah, that's pretty damned funny.

Bryan Cunt. I ain't even been abroad before! Har har har!

The Gaoler passes by. He is a large Sikh

Gaoler All right, boys?

Bryan Fuck off, you different-coloured bastard.

Ralph Careful.
Gaoler Going home soon, Bryan.

The Gaoler passes on

Bryan What you mean "careful". You mean, I might get into trouble?
Ralph I mean, he might come back and knock seven different kinds of shit out of you.
Bryan Hilarious. What is this country anyway? They got Chinks everywhere and they got fucking Pakis running the gaols. Sounds like a pretty fucked-up sort of place to me.
Ralph Sounds just like home.
Bryan What d'*you* know?
Ralph He's not a Paki.
Bryan Well, whatever he is.
Ralph How could he be a Paki?
Bryan What are you gonna tell me—he's a fucking Jap or something?
Ralph He's a Sikh. And it's *not* a surprise to see him here. Wherever you go in the world you find Sikhs in jobs like this—they have a reputation for toughness...
Bryan (*suddenly*) Oh, fucking hell, though, it ain't fair! (*He buries his head in his hands*)

Ralph pulls the headphones of the Walkman over his ears and listens to the music

Don't put that on! Come on, take it off.
Ralph Why?
Bryan I don't know.

Ralph looks at him for a while, then takes it off again. Long silence

I mean, you're carrying on as though this sort of thing is happening to you all the time. I mean, don't pretend you couldn't give a stuff, all right? You gotta be as chewed up about it as I am, haven't you? Unless you want to fucking die, which I doubt.

Ralph says nothing. They look at one another

Ralph Just don't you think of coming up on me when I'm asleep...
Bryan No, no, no...
Ralph I mean it—don't even think of it.
Bryan All right, no need to threaten me.

Ralph I just want to make it clear to you, OK?
Bryan It's clear, it's clear. Fucking hell, touchy, entcha?
Ralph Yeah. I don't like people coming up on me.
Bryan Well, you're in the wrong place, son.

Ralph looks at him

   In here. This is the wrong place for you.
Ralph Just leave me alone.
Bryan Yeah, I'll leave you alone. Just like you left me alone.
Ralph I'm sorry...
Bryan Oh, fucking hell, he's apologising!
Ralph ...But you shouldn't win prizes. (*He laughs at him—a curious, joyless laugh. It's creepy*)

SCENE 2

Hotel, Penang

It is a large, adequately furnished, impersonal hotel room with one or two ethnic touches to distinguish it from other hotel rooms in other parts of the world

George and Wendy come in—Bryan's parents. They are both in their forties, although they both have the worried and hunched bearing of people older than their age. With them is Lilly, Bryan's sister. She is about nineteen— overweight, sluttish, glazed. She carries a very small baby, invariably crying its head off. They have all just arrived after a long flight. Leading the way is the female Lawyer who is handling Bryan's case—Mrs Mahalingam. She is a crisp, well turned-out woman in her thirties or younger. She is an elegant Tamil, speaks excellent English. Wendy and Lilly both have loud, uncompromising voices, George is very quiet. They carry luggage with them

Lawyer Ah, yes, this is it; I think they made a little mistake downstairs, actually.
George Yes, I think so.
Lawyer But I think it's quite clean and comfortable; we've used it before many times...
George Thank you.
Lawyer I think you'll be OK here.
George Very nice, thank you—and thank you for coming all the way out to the airport. I did run a check and I had a reasonable idea of the route in, didn't I, Wendy?

Lawyer Oh, it is no problem.

George Not that we know where we are, do we, Wendy? (*He laughs—a throaty, smoker's laugh*) Never been to this part of the world before, to tell you the——

Lawyer Well you are in Penang island proper; it is separated from the mainland by a short stretch of water with very regular ferries. The city here is known as Georgetown.

George Really? Well, that's suitable, isn't it, 'cos George is my name, see. George in Georgetown. Don't suppose there'll be many Georges as such here, will there? They'll have their own names, won't they? Why is that? Because the British was here—is it?

Lawyer Yes, they were here, very much so.

George I thought so. 'Cos there are a lot of Georgetowns all over the world, aren't there? Jamestowns. Victorias. It's funny how they hang on to those old names after all this time, isn't it? You'd think they'd want to change 'em, you know, sort of get their own names.

The baby is crying

Wendy I think he wants a feed, Lil.

Lilly I know he does.

Wendy I'm just telling you because sometimes you don't seem to realize...

Lilly 'Course I realize—whose baby is it—yours or mine?

Wendy It ain't mine!

Lilly No.

Wendy I finished with all that, girl, bloody ages ago, thank Christ...

Lilly Well, then.

Lawyer Now apparently this is a suite...

George Yes, they told us it was a suite...

Lawyer ...So your room should be through here... Yes.

Lilly Right.

The Lawyer goes ahead to check the adjoining room

George Try and say thank you, Lil, because she's been very kind to us.

Lilly Shut up, you fucking crawler.

Lilly goes with the baby into the next room

George and Wendy are together. George starts looking through a suitcase

George Well, it seems to have everything, dunnit? (*He checks something*) What's this?

Wendy What you bloody talking, Georgetown?

George I'm just being "amickable" with her, aren't I? She's Bry's lawyer— stands to reason we should get on with her.

Wendy "Georgetown—my name's George"—she'll think you're mad. Leave that case; you won't know where to put nothing.

George Oh, I'm bleedin' tired, though, Wend. You reckon it's that jet lag thing I got?

Wendy I dunno what you got, mate, but whatever it is, it ain't worth having.

George What is she, d'you reckon? Only, I always thought Malayans was a darker race.

Wendy Don't rumple all them things up.

George No, I'm just...

Wendy Just don't rumple 'em. They're packed so I know where everything is.

George No, I'm just...

Wendy What you looking for?

George Umm...

Wendy Come on, get out of it. You're worse than her and that kid.

George I thought I'd put me sandals on, only with this tropical climate...

Wendy I'll find 'em for you in a minute. Sit down there. God, I haven't had a decent smoke since we left home. (*She lights up*) Trust you to get us in a no-smoking area on the plane...

George Well, I thought with Lil's kiddie—you know, passive smoking. I was reading about that in the *Sunday Times*...

Wendy You consider me for a change. (*She coughs grotesquely*) God, I needed that. "Passive smoking!" Stupid bastard.

George It was a very interesting drive in, I thought. It's still too early to form a view, sort of thing, but from what I could see—most of the residents appeared to be Chinese. I always thought Malayans were a dark race, somewhat like the Indians. Darker than the Pakis. It's terrible when you come to think of it, though, Wend, what you don't know about the geography of the world we live in.

Wendy I dunno what fucking world you live in; it ain't the same as mine, I'll tell you.

George No, I was just trying to place the Malayans...

Wendy Place 'em in the sea, I would. The bastards.

George Well, we'll see, won't we?

Wendy Seen already, haven't we?

They sit staring into space for a while. George lights up. He has a coughing fit too. Followed by more silence

At last the Lawyer enters

Lawyer Well, your daughter seems to be all right in there.

George Yes, lovely, thank you.

Lawyer You don't seem to have much of a view, I'm afraid...

George No, I was thinking...

Wendy (*stonily*) We don't really want a view, thank you.

Lawyer No.

George So, you'll appreciate we're both very interested to know how Bryan is. I mean, when you last saw him and...

Lawyer Well, obviously he's very upset...

George Yes.

Lawyer ...And a little bitter. I think it's hard for him to take in at the present time...

George Well, it would be hard for anybody, no matter what he's——

Lawyer But as I told you in the car, we have not given up hope. Not by any means.

George Thank you. Well, that's good to hear, isn't it, Wendy?

Wendy says nothing

So what hope can there actually be, would you say? At this moment in time.

Lawyer Well, regarding *Bryan*, let me say—in Bryan's case as distinct from Ralph's—a pardon on appeal is an altogether more feasible prospect. I don't want to raise false hopes, not at all, but I think I can say that. I think that in Court we were able to prove that the nature of their responsibility was quite different. Bryan was duped, there's agreement on that. Ralph is unmistakably the guilty one—he's a member of an international syndicate and all that...

George Is he really? Tsk tsk tsk!

Lawyer But Bryan was different, of course: first offence; not a user or supplier; just a tourist and a dupe on this one single occasion. Also, there is the question of his IQ rating. His IQ being—um—so low, he is the type who is more easily led astray. We were able to prove that in this sense he was led astray. Courts in this part of the world set great store by this sort of evidence, you know...

George Do they, yes—well, if you think it will be a helpful, a chink of light sort of thing...

Lawyer Well, I'm reasonably optimistic about this whole area of our appeal, frankly. It is more likely to be taken notice of on appeal than in Court, oddly enough.

George Yes, I see.

Wendy Sorry, you say his IQ is what? Very low, you say?

Lawyer Well...

Wendy You see, I don't know what you mean by that at all.

George Well, it's his IQ, isn't it?

Lawyer Well, we were able to produce a renowned psychiatrist, you know, who was able to measure it. It's not *chronically* low—please don't get me wrong...

George No no, you have to...

Wendy You mean, he's not very bright. That's what you're trying to say, isn't it?

George No, listen, Wend...

Wendy A psychiatrist? Excuse me, but I got to laugh, quite frankly...

Lawyer Compared to Ralph, certainly—there is a discernible gap. That is the crucial factor. Only IQ-wise, you understand. There is definitely a question of leader and led.

George Yeah, that's what it is, see, Wend. The other boy—what it is with him—well, he's clever, isn't he?

Lawyer Well, he does have a very high rating...

Wendy Oh, he's clever.

Lawyer Anyhow, this is one line we will certainly be taking and frankly I believe we should be grasping at every straw.

George Thank you.

Wendy Yes, well, that's what it is, isn't it? Grasping at straws.

George Well, it's a question of you've got to take every...

Lawyer The law here is very strong on this matter.

Wendy Yeah, well, we have heard, thank you.

George Yes, we have heard.

Lawyer Personally, although the situation is very serious, I believe there are grounds for optimism.

George Thank you very much.

Wendy But it's not your boy, is it?

George No, listen to the lady, Wend...

Wendy So I don't know what you mean you're "optimistic". I mean, it's me that's optimistic or pessimistic, isn't it? I mean, I'm the one who's involved, you know what I mean?

Lawyer (*kindly*) Yes, I know.

Wendy I mean, I know you're probably doing the best you can and you're probably quite a sincere person, but you see, I'm not going to just stand by and let that boy hang, am I? I haven't come all the way out here to attend a hanging.

George I don't think we actually attend...

Wendy I've been in touch with my MP. He's a leading Labour MP and he's taken an interest in our case...

George He's very good.

Wendy He's written letters and made deputations to this that and the other...

George We live in an inner-city area, you know.

Wendy And it's a *personal* interest he's taken, not just so he can get votes...

George He doesn't have to do it; he's already an MP.

Wendy At this moment he's trying to raise the issue with the Queen.

George It's funny, we never went to church at all before this happened. (*He laughs and coughs*)

Wendy The Prime Minister is expected to intervene.

Lawyer Of course, all that is to the good.

George The Prime Minister does usually intervene, isn't that right? As a last resort, sort of thing?

Pause. They ponder this

I expect there'll be some sort of deal going on right now, at top level, sort of thing, won't there? You just don't know, do you?

Lawyer Well, I'll telephone you later—I'd better let you get settled in now.

George Yes, thank you.

Lawyer If there's anything you want to know, anything at all—please don't hesitate to ring me at the office or at home. (*She passes George her card*)

George Oh, thank you... Oh, I see your home address is on the back. That's useful, isn't it? Cor, that's a long name, isn't it?

Lawyer Mrs Mahalingam. But you can call me Katie, if you like—everyone calls me that. It's the nearest thing.

George What is it, a Malayan name, is it?

Lawyer No, it's a Tamil name, actually.

George Oh.

Lawyer India, you know.

George Oh! Oh, I was wondering what you—I was just saying, wasn't I, Wend?

Lawyer Yes, we're simply all over the place.

George You're telling me. I mean, where we come from...

Wendy Thank you—we'll be in touch.

The Lawyer goes

George reads the card

George Mrs Maha... Mahal... I can't even say it, Wend!

Wendy "We live in an inner-city area". You prat.

George What about it?

Wendy You berk.

George Well, we do.

Wendy What's it got to do with anything?

George Well, she's an Indian. She'll know we sort of live amongst 'em. Other Indians and Pakis and that. Which we do live amongst 'em.

Wendy You'd send 'em all back home if you had your way.

George I wouldn't! When did I say that? I ain't never said nothing like that. I might have in jest once or twice. You're talking about in jest.

Wendy All right. Shut up.

George I don't think it can do any harm to tell her that we move amongst her kind.

Wendy Jesus Christ.

George But I do think it's very enlightened of them, though, Wend, to have an Indian as a lawyer. Because they're not in the majority here. If they was, it would be India, wouldn't it? It wouldn't be Malaya at all. Plus the fact she's a woman. How many lawyers are there in England that are Indian *and* women? It would be interesting to know that, Wend. It's funny, ennit? You go abroad and you come across little things like that that really surprise you, you know what I mean? They sort of... (*He mimes surprise*) Don't you think that's enlightened?

Wendy You can't help being enlightened; your head's full of holes.

George (*laughing good-naturedly*) That's good, Wend.

Wendy We haven't come here to be enlightened or observe the various what's-'is-names—we come here because our boy's being hanged! Or has it escaped your attention?

George I know; I suppose I'm just sort of seeking a refuge really.

Wendy Well, don't seek it in stupidity, if you can help it. We got to keep a clear head or they'll treat us like scum. They're just like at home, only worse.

George No, I'm just saying...

Wendy Well, don't say. Don't say nothing. I'm fed up with the sound of your voice. I'm not taking my son home in a box.

George Can you get my pills out of there, because...

Wendy Here.

George Ta. Got the bleedin' shakes already, I have. Which ones is it—I can't see without me glasses... Where's me glasses...? Tell you something else, though, Wend; that girl didn't ought to talk like that to me in front of other people. Did you hear what she said to me? I dunno—ever since she got herself pregnant—her whole manner seems to have altered with me. The things she says. No-one's ever spoken to me the way she does. Except you, but that's normal. I got to have respect, though, Wend—I think I've got to have a word with her. No way can she talk like that to me, specially not in front of strangers.

Wendy She didn't hear.

George I think she did. D'you think she didn't? She probably didn't. But still.

Wendy I don't know where your bloody glasses are. Have I got to think of everything?

George No, it's just these labels, they make 'em so small...

Wendy These are your carba … carba…

George Carbamazepine! That's the ones.

Wendy What a fucking hole, though! Did you see it on the way in? (*She starts unpacking the case*)

George Yeah, I thought it was…

Wendy Bloody shanty-town full of Chinese and they're gonna hang our Bryan. They got a fucking cheek. Oi, Lil!

Lilly comes in, without her baby

Lilly What?

Wendy What you bring this for? (*She holds up a swimming costume from the case*)

Lilly What d'you think?

Wendy You can forget going swimming here, all right?

Lilly Why not?

Wendy 'Cos you're not, that's all.

Lilly They got the sea, haven't they?

Wendy They may have the sea, BUT YOU AIN'T GOING IN IT!

George Shh! Shh!

Lilly (*laughing*) That's that prickly heat you got there.

Wendy FANCY BRINGING THIS, YOU COW!

Lilly WHO YOU CALLING A COW?

George Shh, come on now…

Lilly It's supposed to be the fucking tropics!

George Well, it *is* the tropics, Wend—fair enough. There was a lot of them palm trees on the way in.

Wendy We are here because our Bryan—your brother—has been sentenced to death by a bunch of savages. Can you get that into your thick skull? You an' all. How d'you think it would look in the papers if there was this picture of you swanning about in the water while our Bryan's on death row? They'd love that, wouldn't they?

Lilly All right—I wasn't going to go now—I was going to leave it until after.

Pause. Lilly realizes what she's said

Fuck it.

George I suppose they would print a picture like that, really. I suppose we ought to be on our guard, sort of thing. I hadn't thought of that. I suppose we're newsworthy really, aren't we?

Wendy You always fucking have been. We got to be serious about this, all of us, or they're gonna hang our Bryan. (*She throws the costume back*) It won't fit you no more anyway.

Lilly Nothing does fit me. When am I gonna get my figure back?

Wendy Shouldn't drink so much, should you?

Lilly Look who's talking!

Wendy I am.

Lilly Yeah, look who's talking!

George Don't start rowing—my nerves won't stand it.

Lilly They won't hang him; they wouldn't fucking dare.

Wendy Better hope you're right, girl.

George Er, Lil—just a … before we, er…

Lilly What?

George No, it's just…

Lilly What's the matter with him?

Wendy You've upset him.

Lilly Do what?

Wendy Why don't you mind how you talk to your father?

Lilly Ooh, my "father"!

Wendy Don't put your feet on that; I don't want them complaining about muddy marks.

George No, what it is, Lilly—I'll be quite honest with you…

Lilly Oh, that'll make a change.

George What it is…

Lilly You already said that.

George When that woman was here you had a little go at me, didn't you? It's all right—we're all under pressure, and I expect a little niggle or two will be coming out in the ensuing days. But, well, what it is, you see, Lilly—a family, it's like the insides of a car, you know? Every bit under there depends on every other bit; they can't function if one bit isn't turning over and doing its proper job an' that. That's what a family's like, see? You get one that's out of tune—or "sync" as they call it—well, you've a breakdown, haven't you? Chaos. You have to pull over on to the hard shoulder. You get what I mean? The hard shoulder of life. I mean, I don't blame you—don't get me wrong; we're all under pressure. I'll let it go with a word this time, but I'd really rather you didn't address me like you did just now in front of Mrs Marlgam.

Lilly What d'you know about the insides of a car? I haven't finished that feed yet… (*She starts to go*) I feel like a fucking cow, don't I?

Lilly goes back to her room

Wendy She's grown up very fast, that girl.

George I don't know. She defies her parents.

Wendy Haven't you taken that pill yet?

George You think it's all right to drink the water? Better not, eh? I should've asked Mrs Marlgam.

Wendy Don't be stupid.
George What?
Wendy You don't want to get ill, do you? Which you will get ill if you drink
the water. Don't give 'em the satisfaction. Use the Coke we brought.
George Oh, yeah. (*He goes to the bathroom with a large bottle of Coca Cola*)
Wendy (*stubbing out her cigarette*) Got to think of everything round here.

SCENE 3

The prison cell

*Ralph and the Gaoler are playing chess. Bryan is absent. Ralph has his
headset on; his foot is slowly keeping beat. He and the Gaoler are smoking
marijuana—passing the joint to and fro. There is still the soft clamour from
the other rooms—but there is a cool laid-back atmosphere*

*The Gaoler has to summon enormous resources of concentration to play.
Ralph takes down his headset*

Ralph Wait a minute—you're moving your king into check.
Gaoler Pardon?
Ralph Your king. You're in check there from my bishop. See?
Gaoler Oh. Never mind.
Ralph What d'you mean, never mind? You can't move your king into check.
Gaoler I will move him away next time.
Ralph Are you sure you've played this game before?
Gaoler Oh, yes—I am the champion round here.
Ralph I'd like to meet the opposition.
Gaoler I play Punjabi rules.
Ralph Even in Punjab you can't move your king into check.
Gaoler Maybe.
Ralph Definitely.
Gaoler You're too good for me, Ralph. Here—it has gone out... (*He passes
him the joint*)
Ralph Thanks...
Gaoler Your hand is not shaking at all.
Ralph No.
Gaoler The other one, Bryan—he is going all to pieces.
Ralph He's young.
Gaoler That has nothing to do with it, believe me. I have seen big men—
tough, you know... (*he mimes "goes to pieces"*) He got you caught.

Ralph shrugs

He is a racist.

Ralph He hasn't had time to become anything else.

Gaoler But here everything is forgiven. Here you can say anything. You know why I am good at my job?

Ralph Because you're a big hairy sadistic bastard.

Gaoler (*laughing*) No! Well, maybe, a little. But no, I am good at my job because I am indifferent on the question of abuse. Really, it is all water off the duck's back. You can only do your work properly and well if you are indifferent.

Ralph Yes. You know, when it comes to the moment—I expect to have no feeling whatsoever. Just as I've never had any feeling about any person. Not for the people whose lives I've ruined. They *say* I've ruined.

Gaoler Well, we give you a drug, you know—to deaden the feelings.

Ralph I won't need it.

Gaoler It is not compulsory. We can get you some cocaine, if you like.

Ralph (*amused*) Really?

Gaoler Yes, just be sure to place your order, in good time.

Ralph So you'll smuggle it in?

Gaoler Yes. In here. (*He taps his turban*) Better than the underpants!

Ralph I'd like to see that, but I don't think I'll even need that.

Gaoler Oh, you will panic like anything when it comes to it. They all do.

SCENE 4

The prison visiting room

Bryan is the only prisoner being visited. He is there opposite Wendy, George and Lilly with the baby. Bryan is chained at the wrists. A Gaoler sits close by

Wendy I'm very, very upset about this, though, Bryan, I am really.

Bryan Well, I ain't exactly over the moon about it, am I?

Wendy Soon as you won that bleedin' prize I knew there'd be trouble, didn't I, George?

George Well...

Wendy And look at your hair—what have they done to it?

Bryan Never mind that. You spoken to a lawyer or not?

Wendy Yeah, she came out to the airport, didn't she?

George Mrs Marlgam...

Bryan I don't mean her. For fuck's sake, she couldn't get you off a parking fine. I mean a proper English lawyer.

Wendy Well, in England, yeah—didn't we, George?

George Oh, yeah, we...

Bryan What did he say?

Wendy Well, he said—but it's the MP really that we hold out the most hope for, isn't it, George?

George What, Chris?

Wendy Yeah.

George (*to Bryan*) I call him Chris, like, because he said we ought to, didn't he? He's not a bit like an MP—he's...

Bryan What did he say?

George Well, he's very interested...

Bryan Interested! I'm "interested" but there's fuck-all I can do about anything.

Wendy He might even come out here, but for the moment he's trying to raise it in the House of Parliament.

George Yeah, it's a sort of special what's-'is-name—privilege or something whereby he can raise it in the House. What's it called, a filibuster or something...

Wendy Something like that.

George I got a book on it indoors...

Bryan Book! You ain't got a fucking book on what I got in here. You ain't got a bloody video on it neither. *Midnight Express*? This is ten times as bad.

Wendy The bastards.

George I think perhaps you'd better keep your voice down, Bry.

Bryan Yeah? What they gonna do? Fine me? Give me an 'undred lines?

Wendy He's got to shout, hasn't he? Let off steam a bit.

George Yeah, I know, but... I dunno.

Bryan You should see the poxy food they got in here. Fucking pigswill, 'cept they wouldn't give it to pigs. I've had the running shits ever since I come in here.

George Oh, that's no joke, that isn't.

Bryan What you gonna do for me, then? Eh?

Wendy We're going to get you out of here, Bryan...

Bryan 'Cos they can't carry this out, can they? It's outrageous. Tell 'em this: number one—I'm a minor; I ain't twenty-one. Number two—I was led astray by a fucking syndicate on threat of my life. Number three—I'm English. Number four—they didn't ought to hang people for this sort of crime. I don't think that Paki tart got all that across, specially about being led astray on fear of my life an' that. Hanging! I couldn't believe my fucking ears. I thought they was having me on.

George It could be they was just trying to scare you, Bry.

Bryan Well, they fucking succeeded.

George It could be that, couldn't it, Wend?

Wendy I'm so upset I don't know what to think.

George See, it could be they proceed as though they got every intention of carrying out the what's-'is-name, the sentence, then at the last minute they say "All right, we let you off".

Bryan Yeah. You reckon?

George They used to do that. It's in history, you know. Chris reckons it's a possibility, don't he, Wend?

Bryan What, he said that, did he?

George Yeah. Well, it was sort of off the record, like. He can't make that sort of information public, can he?

Bryan Only it's completely outrageous. I ain't hardly done nothing.

George No. Well, it was heroin, Bryan.

Wendy Oh, shut up, George.

Bryan I know it was fucking heroin.

George No, I'm just saying—if we're going to help him, we've got to face the facts. That's all I'm saying.

Bryan I know it was fucking heroin!

George All right—shh!

Bryan But it was only twelve ounces.

George No, it's just that I saw this programme—d'you remember watching it, Wend?

Bryan Very nice for you.

George No, but some of the things they showed about the results of heroin and that. I mean, it wasn't sensationalised—it was quite educational, really. God, they got these little kids with…

Wendy Shut up.

Bryan Give it a fucking rest.

They all sit there, lost in their thoughts for some time

(*To Lilly*) All right?

Lilly No so bad.

Bryan How's the baby, then?

Lilly He's all right.

Bryan Where's Gary?

Lilly Dunno. Don't care neither.

Bryan What, it's all over, is it?

Lilly shrugs

Good riddance, eh?

George Oh, have you mentioned the papers?

Wendy How could I have when you been with me all the time?

George No, I thought you might have…

Wendy You been here with me—you heard every word I said.

George Suppose I have. (*He laughs and coughs*)
Bryan What papers?
Wendy We'll talk about it another time…
Bryan Talk about it now.
Lilly They sold their story to the Sunday papers.
Wendy Do you mind?
Lilly No.
Bryan What story?
Wendy Do-you-mind?
Lilly No.
Bryan What story?
Wendy Thank you very much.
Lilly 'S all right.
Wendy Go and tell the whole place—go on.
Lilly It was him that brought it up.
Bryan Shut up. What story?
George Well, it's the story of—everything really…
Bryan What story you got? You ain't got a fucking story.
George Well, what it is really, Bry—it's a sort a hin-depth account—more of an account than a story—about you as a child and young man an' that…
Bryan Oh, charming.
George I think it will be quite sensitively handled on the whole really.
Bryan I bet you do. How much they giving you for that?
George Well, a final figure has yet to be…
Lilly Ten thousand pounds.
Bryan Fucking hell.
Wendy Would you go and wait outside, please?
Lilly No.
Bryan You done all right for yourselves, ain't you? Considering you haven't got a story. I'm the one with the story, not you. Childhood? Mine only lasted ten minutes.
George We appreciate everything you say, Bryan, but if you could just keep your voice down…
Bryan Ah, yeah, but I'll be dead, won't I? So I can't tell my story! Fucking tasty—I thought you was coming out here to help me, turns out it's so you can sell your story.
George We couldn't have come without it, Bry.
Bryan Fucking tasty. Proper cunt I'm going to look, aren't I, swinging at the end of a rope and you lot poncing off to Spain. I suppose it won't happen if I get off, will it?
George Oh, yeah. Won't it, Wend? We checked that, didn't we, and they told us there was that clause.
Wendy Shut your mouth.

George You got to be realistic, Bryan…

Bryan Oh, don't worry about that; I'm realistic in here. It's getting realer every day.

George No, how d'you think we could of afforded it, coming out here?

Bryan I thought the Government paid.

George No, Bryan—the paper paid. What's the harm in that?

Bryan What's the harm? I'll tell you what's the harm … if you don't know I can't tell you. Only I hope you'll have the decency to let the body get cold before it comes out.

Wendy has started to cry

George It's all right, Wend—it's just family talk. Ennit, Bry?

Bryan Family talk? (*He scoffs*) No such thing, is there? All fucking grunts, ennit? Come on—don't cry; they enjoy it when you start that in here. Think they've won, don't they?

Wendy I'm very, very upset about it all.

Lilly You already said that.

Wendy Seeing you in here. Christ almighty.

George We did leave you some personal effects at the desk. I didn't know what the position was regarding them, so…

Bryan What did you bring?

George Brought you some fags, toothpaste, biscuits, some soap. Brought you some magazines. Anything else, you just let us know, all right? I expect we're allowed to bring in food really.

Bryan (*to Wendy*) Shut up, will you? Fucking depressing, having someone crying all the time. (*To George*) Toilet paper.

George Toilet paper? Yeah, all right, Bry, toilet paper. Yeah, come on, Wend—chin up, eh? We got to be positive, haven't we, Bry?

Bryan Yeah.

George The Arsenal's winning anyway. That new bloke's fitting in all right. He does some clever things, but I still think they was wrong to sell Charlie…

Bryan Oh, fuck off.

Bryan suddenly gets up and goes

The Gaoler looks confused but follows

Wendy Bryan! You come back here and say goodbye! Bryan!

Bryan sticks his head round the door. He doesn't look at them, but raises a hand

Bryan Yeah, bye…

Bryan goes

Wendy In chains.
George Yeah. You don't think he has to have 'em on all the time, do you? I'll ask.
Wendy Bloody chained up like an animal or something.
George Yeah, well, worse than an animal, isn't it?
Wendy Bloody Arabs, they're all bloody barbarians. It's enough to turn you into a racialist. Come on, let's get out of here.
George Yeah, come on…
Wendy Don't you ever let me cry like that again. I'm never going to cry again—d'you hear me? I didn't hardly see him. (*She speaks to Lilly in a new, harsh voice*) You comin' or you want them to keep you here an' all?

They go, followed by Lilly

SCENE 5

The prison cell

Bryan is alone, lying on the bunk, reading boxing magazines

The Gaoler comes in

Bryan What?
Gaoler I am to keep you company.
Bryan I don't want any company, do I?
Gaoler How are you? (*He sits down, intent upon staying*)
Bryan Oh, for fuck's sake. I got all them out there to talk to, haven't I?
Gaoler They are other prisoners.
Bryan Yeah, well, I prefer other prisoners, all right?
Gaoler They do not speak your language. Except for the German boy and he is elsewhere.
Bryan Yeah, well…
Gaoler It was not a very useful interview with your parents, I think?

Bryan scoffs and says nothing

It is most upsetting when a family cannot sit down and speak with one another. I have seen something of this and have taken great care to make sure I always speak properly to my sons.

Bryan Well, that's bully for you, ennit? Look, I got all these magazines, haven't I? I'm quite happy—or I was till you come in here.
Gaoler OK.
Bryan Thank you very much.
Gaoler I must remember I am not social worker; I am only prison guard.
Bryan Fucking hell, don't send a social worker in here; I got enough problems.

Pause. The Gaoler doesn't go

All right, tell you what: say if you had to bet, sort of thing. You know, if you had to bet your life on it ... what would you say's gonna happen? Is this sentence gonna be carried out, d'you reckon?
Gaoler You are asking me for hope.
Bryan No, no, I'm just asking you a straight question...
Gaoler If I had to bet my life—I cannot imagine being in such an extreme situation as this; it is completely, er ... hypothetical...
Bryan All right, forget it. Forget I asked, if you can't answer a simple straightforward question.
Gaoler I think you should make your peace.
Bryan Right. See, you can answer. It's not difficult, is it? I see. You reckon, then?
Gaoler I am saying you should make your peace in any case, regardless of what happens.
Bryan Yeah, well, that doesn't apply, does it? Because I'm not religious.
Gaoler I know.
Bryan You know that—you know everything, don't you?
Gaoler Religion would be useful but not essential. I am not actually speaking about religion; I am speaking about you, within yourself. You have a golden opportunity, which very few of us ever get: you can achieve if you like a kind of greatness.
Bryan A kind of what? Greatness?
Gaoler A greatness of spirit.
Bryan What, in here?
Gaoler In here especially. Perhaps only.
Bryan They better start feeding us properly first.
Gaoler Most people's lives, what are they? Nothing. They come and they go; they do not even disturb the ripples on the pond of the world. They are never tested. You have now the supreme test; it is happening to you now.
Bryan Is that a fact?
Gaoler You should let——
Bryan Yeah, well, why don't we forget it, yeah?
Gaoler ——You should let your ego break free. Let it go where your body cannot.

Bryan OK, I give it up. D'you see it? It went out the window—you missed it! I'll give up smoking an' all.

Gaoler Where I come from a boy of twelve has more spirituality than you.

Bryan Yeah? Well, why didn't you fucking stay there. Pakis are always going on about "Where I come from" and all that. Yet they can't wait to get away from their own bloody country, can they?

Gaoler There is poison in your head—you should try to release it...

Bryan Oi—I'm a dangerous man, all right? They reckon you're a hard man. 'Cos you're some special breed of Paki or something. You know what? I don't think you are at all. You don't look it to me—you certainly don't talk like it. You talk like a poof, if you really wanna know. Know what I mean, a poof, a faggot? You wanna be more careful, going into people's cells like this. I'm a dangerous prisoner.

Gaoler Yes, you have been a danger to society.

Bryan No, I am now. I still am—highly dangerous. Stands to reason, dunnit? Else why are they hanging me?

Pause

Fucking boring in here, I'll tell you. Is that what you come in here for, Mushtapha? Bit of aggravation, was it? Stir up the prisoners? Come on, then.

Gaoler What are you doing?

Bryan Come on, see who's best. It don't matter to me, does it? Come on, you foreign fucker. (*He smacks the Gaoler round the face. He starts dancing round him, moving like a boxer and smacking his face. He laughs with each blow. The blows get harder—they ring out*)

The Gaoler follows him and waits. At last Bryan lunges with a dangerous punch, the Gaoler dodges it, gets behind him and pins both his arms. It is ridiculously easy for him. Bryan cries out in pain

All right, all right... Take it easy...

The Gaoler lets him go

You broke my fucking arm; I heard a crack, you bastard. That's fucking wrestling, that what you did. I was boxing. Don't you know the difference? Why couldn't you stick to the rules, once in a while?

Gaoler Come on, it's OK. Shake.

Bryan Fuck off.

Gaoler We'll shake later. Hard man.

Bryan I was boxing! Anyone can bloody wrestle.

Gaoler Ah, well, you are on the wrong side to make the rules, Bryan.

Bryan I distinctly heard a crack… What wrong side? What you talking about? Wrong side of what? The law, I suppose.

Gaoler Not only that.

Bryan You gotta be the weirdest prison guard ever, man.

Gaoler (*laughing*) Yes, I am pretty weird, aren't I?

Bryan I could report you—I hope you realize that. Smoking dope in here with prisoners.

Gaoler Ah, well, then I would *definitely* break the rules.

Bryan Wouldn't make any difference to me, would it?

Gaoler You would be surprised. Oh, standards must be falling quite dramatically, if that is how Englishmen talk these days.

Bryan Bollocks fucking Englishmen. There ain't no such thing no more ever since we let your lot in.

Ralph comes in. Perhaps he is still wearing his wrist chains—in which case he is unchained now

What's the matter with you, shit-for-brains?

Ralph Huh?

Bryan "Huh!?" You look as though you seen a ghost.

Ralph (*spookily*) Maybe that's just what I did see!

Bryan Shut up.

Ralph I just received the official visit. My mother.

Gaoler Ah, very nice!

Bryan She upset, was she?

Ralph Well, my mother doesn't get upset. I mean, she pretends to be. That's not the point. I'm just very honoured, that's all. We all are, most honoured. (*He sits down*)

Gaoler Absolutely. This is most true. Our mothers are jewels of the sky, our number one asset in life.

Ralph closes his eyes under the headset

Bryan Fucking funny farm, this is.

SCENE 6

The hotel. Toni's room, similar to George and Wendy's. It is early evening

Toni is Ralph's mother, but she's in her early forties. She looks glamorous and has an even tan. She looks like a nouveau riche. At the start she is in bed

Beside her, still asleep, is a young Malay—actually the Barman at the hotel—although this is not clear until he puts his clothes on

Toni checks her watch. When she speaks it is with a Lancashire accent, but it has an affected drawl that she probably thinks is posh

Toni Oh God… Come on! Come on, wakey-wakey! Yes—you. Come on, the bell tolls.

Barman wakes, mumbling

I know, yes, come on…

Barman asks something

Never mind that. Don't ruin this beautiful silence with questions. You've got to go. Come on, love, be a good boy and get yourself dressed.

He gets out of bed. He is about twenty years younger than her—a very desirable hunk. She admires him from the bed

Mm, did you really cop that, Toni? Not losing your touch, are you?
Barman Hm?
Toni Nothing, love, come on—chop-chop.
Barman Not chop-chop.
Toni All right, scram, skadoodle, on your bike or in your rickshaw, whatever it is. Oh, you young boys—you're so hard to get shot of. An older man would be so grateful he'd run for it, but you have to… Go on, get your hands out me hair. Go on—get yourself dressed; I'm expecting someone.
Barman Here?
Toni Yes, of course here.
Barman OK. (*He gets dressed*)

She watches him for a moment. By this time we realize he is an employee at the hotel—he puts on a bow-tie and white jacket, etc.

See you again, yeah?
Toni Again?
Barman Yeah. Maybe later, OK?
Toni Your way of asking, it's perfect rapture.
Barman Sure.
Toni Go on now and polish your buttons.

He is dressed by now

You're fast at getting dressed, aren't you? Had plenty of practice, I expect.
Eh! Don't forget your tray.

Barman Ah! (*He picks up the tray—it still has some drinks on it*)

Toni You can leave the drinks, love.

Barman You had yours already.

Toni I know, I'll take the others as well.

Barman They are for Room 421.

Toni I'll see they get them. Just put them down there. Pop everything on the
bill, will you, love?

Barman Bill?

Toni It's all right; I'm just having you on, pet. Joking, you know.

Barman Yeah, English women always kidding around.

Toni We have to, love; it's a cry for help.

Barman Cry for help, I come fast.

Toni I know that, love. See you in the bar.

Barman OK. (*He stands for a moment and adjusts his hair—not because it's
ruffled, but because he's vain*)

Toni smiles. There is a knock on the door

You want me hide in the closet?

Toni Certainly not. Open the door.

He opens the door

The Lawyer is there

Barman Hi, come on in!

Lawyer Oh, is this...?

Toni Hallo, Katie, come on; I was expecting you. Thank you! (*She raises her
glass to the Barman*)

The Barman goes

Hallo, love, I just had to have a drink.

Lawyer You're lucky, there have been all kinds of complaints about the
room service here.

Toni Oh, I haven't got any complaints, not yet.

Lawyer So have you had some sleep?

Toni Off and on, you know. (*She is out of the bed, beginning to get dressed*)

*There is a pair of her pants way over the other side of the room. The Lawyer
notices them*

Oh, I just throw my clothes anywhere, that's me. Sorry, I'm not quite ready for you...

Lawyer It's OK; I don't want to push you. I just came to tell you it's perfectly all right for you to see Ralph tomorrow.

Toni Oh, I've seen him.

Lawyer Really? But surely you missed the visiting hours.

Toni I know I did, but they were very obliging. I, um, gave them a little breakdown, you know—very maternal and all that. Men can never resist a woman's tears, can they?

Lawyer Still, I'm surprised.

Toni Well, there's usually a gentleman, isn't there? No matter where you go in the world. You know, I think they're all gentlemen really, at heart. You've just got to bring it out. Yes, there's always one. I'll just get dressed and we'll go downstairs, OK? Help yourself to one of those drinks; I don't know what they are but you might find something you like.

Toni goes to her bathroom

The Lawyer looks at the tray of drinks

SCENE 7

The hotel bar

It is a sterile sort of room, with one or two ethnic knickknacks. There is a well-stocked bar, where the Barman (from the previous scene) is working—cutting up lemons, cleaning tables, etc.

The only customer at the moment is Lilly. She is seated on a stool at the bar, slumped, smoking. She has a beer. She's fed-up, half-drunk. But she can't help admiring the Barman, she watches him as he moves about, although she is careful never to let him notice

Lilly (*finally*) Excuse me. Can I have another, please?

Barman Same again?

Lilly You haven't got no English beer, have you?

Barman Er ... sometimes we got Guinness.

Lilly Oh, yeah? Guinness. Guinness is good for you!

Barman Huh?

Lilly Guinness is good for you! Didn't you know that?

Barman We're out of it right now. I could look in the other bar...

Lilly No no no, you stay there, don't worry. I'll have what I had last time.

I feel like something cold, don't I? Something long and cold, know what I mean?

Barman I don't know.
Lilly No, I don't actually like Guinness.
Barman We don't have Guinness.
Lilly No, I know—it's all right, come on.
Barman You want same again?
Lilly Yeah. Is it always as hot as this?
Barman Hot?
Lilly Yeah, I'm saying—is it always as hot as this?
Barman This is the rainy season right now.
Lilly Yeah? It's always the rainy season at home.
Barman Excuse me, I can't understand what you say. Are you English?
Lilly 'Course I'm English.
Barman You staying upstairs, yeah?
Lilly That's right—in Room 433, got it? 433.
Barman How you like?
Lilly I like it. You mean the room? The room's all right—I wondered what you was talking about there. It's all right. But we ain't here to have a good time, are we? Do you understand?
Barman Er, sure—I don't know.
Lilly No, we're here to have a bad time, see. It's not a holiday—comprendo? I mean, it's only right, really, ennit? (*She drinks*)

The Barman watches her thoughtfully for a while

Barman Hey.
Lilly What?
Barman Hey, you wanna score?
Lilly Wanna score; what d'you mean—score what?
Barman I don't know.
Lilly Sorry, I'm not with you... You mean my room number?
Barman 433, yeah, I got it.
Lilly Well...
Barman I can get you H. You know. (*He mimes needle in arm*) I can get you cocaine; I can get grass, whatever you want.

Lilly looks at him then laughs ironically

It's not me, you know, but I can get it. You just tell me. What's so goddamned funny? Did I say something funny?
Lilly Yeah, you did, as a matter of fact.
Barman OK, crazy.

Lilly Yeah, it's crazy, ennit, pal? The whole fucking thing's crazy, ennit?
Barman OK, you want something, I'm around. Tell your husband.
Lilly My husband, eh? (*She laughs*)
Barman I don't understand you.
Lilly Well, I understand you, so that's all right, ennit?

The Barman tires of her and goes away—but he remains on stage

(*To herself*) Tell your husband! It's a fucking laugh, ennit? (*She lights another cigarette. She coughs*)

The Lawyer and Toni come in. Toni is well-dressed now—lots of chains and jewellery, etc. She makes quite an impression—or she would if the bar were to be crowded

At the start, Lilly doesn't see them and the Barman is away in another area of the stage. The two women make straight for a table

Toni (*coming in*) No, have you ever tried to fly from Marbella to Penang in a hurry?
Lawyer I can't say I have...
Toni Take my advice, love—don't... We'll sit here, shall we? I feel as though I've been through a spin-dryer. I had to leave in such a hurry—I could only leave a note for Steven—that's my husband, you know. Ralph's stepfather. He's away on business as usual.
Lawyer What's his line?
Toni Oh, well, he, um, diversifies. He moves around a lot. What you having, love?
Lawyer I'm not really a drinking lady...
Toni Oh, go on, keep me company.
Lawyer ...But I think perhaps after a hard day.
Toni That's the way.
Lawyer I'll get them. (*To distant Barman*) Excuse me? Excuse me. Tsk, I know he can hear me...
Toni (*without raising her voice*) Waiter.

The Barman comes over

Good evening. I'll have a Jack Collins—can you make one?
Barman Er...
Toni Well, go and look it up in your book, love. A Jack Collins for me and...?
Lawyer I'll have a Tiger.
Toni A what?

Barman You got it.

Toni All right—a Tiger for my friend's tank. And bring some nuts or something, will you please?

Barman Nuts?

Toni Yes, nuts.

The Barman goes

I think he's more at his ease with room service.

Lawyer He does have an insolent way about him. It's because we are women.

Toni Well, I think the young should be insolent; they must find the rest of us so boring. Do you smoke, Katie?

Lawyer No, thank you.

Toni Good girl. (*She lights up. Coughs*) No, I've always kept on the move, you know. Still and running water, and all that. I feel it's best that way, what with my temperament. That poor boy's just the same, a rolling stone. But the problem with Ralph, I think, is that he's got the restless nature but he's never had the energy to go with it. And you need one for the other, don't you?

Lawyer It's a perfect tragedy, isn't it?

Toni What, about Ralph? Mm. (*She brings out a tiny handkerchief and dabs her eyes with it. It is a dubious, theatrical gesture*)

The Lawyer watches her

Still, there you are; we all do these things. There's only one way to stay out of trouble in life and that's stop at home in front of the telly, isn't it? And I'm afraid Ralph broke the golden rule, didn't he?

Lawyer What's that?

Toni Don't get caught.

Lawyer Ah, yes.

Toni I mean to say, really. Having smack in your pants at Penang airport—you've only got to read the papers. It's almost as though he was wanting to get caught, d'you know what I mean?

Lawyer It was a most unnecessary risk.

Toni Well, there you are. But I told him, I said to him—you've always been unworldly, just like your father.

Lawyer When did you say this to him?

Toni This afternoon. His name was Jack Collins, you know—his father. That's why I drink them. It's all that's left of poor old Jack, an old bat sat drinking cocktails in Marbella.

The Barman brings the drinks

Ah, speak of the devil. The devil drink. That looks as though it might have some resemblance to what I asked for. Well done, young man.
Barman I worked in the States for a year.
Toni Oh, a Tiger's a beer, is it? That's a good idea...
Barman Nuts.
Toni Oh, yes, thank you.

The Barman's insolent presence has irritated the Lawyer. She mutters something stern to him in Malay. He goes, swinging away

Eh, I think you said the wrong thing to him there, Katie. You know, I bet you're a handful when you're crossed; I bet you are.
Lawyer I don't like him.
Toni You don't have to, do you? He's only a skivvy.
Lawyer (*smiling*) I had forgotten that word.
Toni Here's to better times!
Lawyer Better times!

Pause while they drink

Toni I'm a monkey; that's why I always ask for nuts.
Lawyer Sorry?
Toni I was born in the year of the monkey. You know, the Chinese calendar. What are you?
Lawyer I've really no idea.
Toni Horse, I'd say.
Lawyer You can tell these things?
Toni Oh, yes—you're definitely a horse.
Lawyer Perhaps I should ask him to bring me some oats.
Toni Oats! Eh, that's very good, love. Oh, thank God I've got a lawyer who's a human being.
Lawyer Actually, I am not like this at all; I'm very stuffy.
Toni (*going straight on*) Now I'll tell you what I was thinking, shall I?
Lawyer Sorry?
Toni I want to put my proposition to you.
Lawyer Oh, yes. Please.
Toni (*her manner has changed*) Now I don't want you to get the wrong idea about me, all right? I don't want you to think I'm trying to shock you or anything. This is strictly business. But I do want to know what you think.
Lawyer OK.
Toni Now as I understand it, the appeal has to go through two stages. First to the Parliament, then to the Governor. And you say the first usually fails, all right...

Lawyer I'm afraid so…

Toni Now the Governor. It'll then be up to him, right?

Lawyer His decision is very crucial.

Toni Quite. (*She eats a nut*) And he'll be a man, of course?

Lawyer Oh, yes.

Toni Now I believe, Katie, that in life each of us should play to our strengths and disguise our weaknesses, you know. I mean, if you're rich, for example, you should use your money. You'd be soft not to. If you're very strong—and so on. (*She eats another nut*) I wonder if I could get to see him?

Lawyer The Governor? It's possible he would give you an appointment.

Toni Hm. He hangs my son and it's possible he'd give me an appointment. Never mind—what was I saying? Yes, I'm going to put it to you straight, Katie, because you've got a lot of human qualities and, well, because there's no-one else, quite frankly.

Lawyer OK.

Toni What if I managed to get to see this Governor at his office—maybe even his home—and I offered myself to him? I mean, I think I'm justified in thinking he'd find me reasonably attractive, don't you?

Lawyer I'm not sure you're serious.

Toni You don't think it's a good idea?

Lawyer You want to—but it doesn't work like that at all.

Toni What doesn't, love?

Lawyer Why, the legal system.

Toni I'm not talking about the legal system, am I? I'm talking about an older system than that. The world is run by men, Katie, with all due respect to your good self. And let's face it, men want one thing and one thing only.

Lawyer Are you really serious?

Toni Absolutely.

Lawyer You want to flirt around with the *Governor*?

Toni Well, that's putting it very demurely; I'm a little surprised at you, Katie.

Lawyer Oh, *you're* surprised at *me*?

Toni I'll give him what he wants and he gives me what I want.

Lawyer The Governor is a married man with grown-up children and everything.

Toni laughs

He's a Muslim.

Toni (*laughing louder*) Don't Muslims do it, then?

Lawyer I've never heard anything so outrageous in all my life.

Toni No, well, you're young yet. I thought I'd just float the idea, you know.

Lawyer I don't believe I'm hearing this, actually.

Toni Don't get me wrong, love; I'm not saying it's something I'd enjoy doing. I expect it would be pretty nasty. I can just imagine what he's like. But we are talking about a human life, aren't we? If it were anything else it would be a different matter. My own son.

Lawyer But what a... Look, I've lived in England, you know. I studied at Cambridge and everything, so I know about the English sense of humour— but assuming you're serious—assuming that, I say... What a very low opinion you must have of us! I mean to say, would you consider such a step if it was in England?

Toni Ah, well, it doesn't quite hold up, that argument, I'm afraid, love, because in England we've done away with the death penalty, haven't we? For better or worse. But what I think is—if you are dealing with barbarians you've got to use barbarian tactics.

Lawyer Barbarians.

Toni says nothing. She eats a nut

You know this is a terrible insult.

Toni It's just between you and me; I did warn you. Why are you taking it personally?

Lawyer I am a member of the society you are insulting.

Toni Are you?

Lawyer Yes.

Toni People can say anything about England to me, I don't bat an eye. Silly, isn't it? All right, come on—forget I said anything. (*She drinks*)

Lawyer But I would say you also have a very low opinion of women.

Toni You're probably dead right there, love.

Lawyer To debase yourself like that; to even think of it. Excuse me, but to use sex in that way...

Toni Well, there's quite a bit of it about, you know. Sex. They use it here, don't they? It's only using what I've got to get what I want. To save a life.

Lawyer Well, it wouldn't work.

Toni All right.

Lawyer We do have a legal system, you know.

Toni Yes, well, you've got the British to thank for that, haven't you?

Lawyer (*bowing*) Thank you very much.

Toni No, you stick to the textbook, love, and you're doomed; the law is just one big textbook, isn't it? It's like that guerrilla warfare, what I'm talking about. If you don't do something—underhand—you're buggered, aren't you? I'll have another, please. (*She signals to the Barman*) You're not keeping up with your Tiger, love.

Lawyer I feel like crying.

Toni Ah. (*She eats a nut*) That's another woman's guile, isn't it?

Lawyer You have a very cynical view of women.

Toni Ooh, you should hear me once I get started on men. He's a Muslim, you say?

Lawyer Hm?

Toni This Governor chappie. You say he's a Muslim. Does he have ten wives?

Lawyer You are thinking of another country entirely.

Toni Am I? Ooh, my geography's terrible.

Lawyer You know I should walk out of that door.

Toni says nothing

But I won't because I think you need me. I think you need me very much.

Toni (*blandly*) Yes.

Lawyer You know I'm very sorry you've raised this—topic, because I wanted you to listen to what I had to say about Ralph and Bryan.

Toni Oh, yes?

From now on, Lilly listens to what is said

Lawyer Well, first—in Ralph's case, as distinct from Bryan's case, I should say that there is a somewhat better chance of a successful appeal.

Toni Really? How's that?

Lawyer Well, you know Ralph is a registered addict. The amount he had on him was very small and I believe in Court we were able to prove that it was for his personal use. They didn't believe it, but they couldn't altogether discount it. Of course, he was with Bryan—who had a substantial amount, and Ralph was a member of a syndicate—that's undeniable, but what I'm saying is there's some hope there.

Toni (*after a beat*) A registered addict.

Lawyer Hm?

Toni Ralph's a registered addict, you say?

Lawyer Yes.

Toni Of heroin? I didn't know that. The things you find out, eh?

Lawyer Well, it may sound strange, but it is all to the good for us at this juncture.

Toni Oh, the appeal, yes.

Lawyer Also, and perhaps more hopefully—I guess you'll know that lawyers and judges can do a lot of behind-the-scenes work? Well, this is not definite, you know, but it's certain that Ralph knows more about this syndicate than he is telling. He knows who is at the head of it and everything. In court he categorically refused to name names, but—well, I believe the door is still open for him.

Toni You mean, all he has to do is name the Mr Big sort of thing?

Lawyer Yes, here in Malaysia. That's what they want.
Toni And he's refused to?
Lawyer Yes, so far.
Toni And if he names him they'll let him off?
Lawyer Nothing is certain. It won't do us any harm.
Toni (*to Barman*) Have you got that Jack Collins yet, please? I'll speak to him.
Lawyer Good.
Toni If that's the way it works, the "system".
Lawyer It's the same in every country; deals are made.
Toni Yes.
Lawyer In England too.
Toni Yes, I'm sure. (*She smiles at her*)
Lawyer Well, I suppose, I'd better be pushing off—my husband will be home.
Toni Oh, I hope it's not too late for you to get to the shops.
Lawyer Thank you for the drink.
Toni Oh, the Tiger, yes. It's all right; I'm glad I was able to tempt you.

The Lawyer looks at her curiously, she can't make Toni out. Toni smiles back

Until tomorrow, then.
Lawyer Yes. Don't worry, hm?
Toni Thank you so much.

Their goodbye is interrupted by the Barman, who comes over and serves Toni her drink. Toni thanks him

The Lawyer leaves

Lilly is now watching Toni. She's a bit wobbly on her stool

Ah, yes, just put it down there, will you?

The Barman allows his hand to pass across her shoulder as he walks away. Toni shows no sign of noticing. Lilly now comes over to Toni's table. She is none too sure of her footing and slurs a bit

Lilly Hallo.
Toni Oh, hallo...
Lilly All right?
Toni Yes, I'm all right.
Lilly D'you mind if I...?

Toni gestures for her to sit down. She does so and immediately seems to enter a reverie

   Sorry, I'm Bryan's sister.
Toni Oh, I see, I wondered... How do you do? I'm Ralph's mother. Well, I expect you know that.
Lilly Yeah. Sorry, I've had a few.
Toni It's all right, love.
Lilly Look like piddle but they don't half go to your head. Still—eh?
Toni Yes. So are you here with your parents?
Lilly Yeah. They're upstairs looking after my kid. (*She doesn't expand on this but she stretches out her legs and arms and heaves a sigh of relief*)

Toni watches her

   (*Finally*) I haven't got a husband.
Toni It's all right, love; it's got nothing to do with me.
Lilly No, I'm just saying. I ain't got anybody. (*She laughs oddly*) How d'you fancy that? (*She nods at the Barman*)

Toni says nothing

   I had a boyfriend, obviously. That's obvious, ennit? You know what he done, him?
Toni Who, your boyfriend?
Lilly No, *him*. (*She indicates the Barman*)
Toni No.
Lilly I was sat over there, having a drink, right? He comes up, he goes "Hey, you want heroin?"

Toni says nothing but she takes this in

   Yeah, I was sitting there—straight, he only offers me heroin, cocaine, hash, I dunno what.
Toni Really?
Lilly You know what I thought? I thought—what's Bryan dying for? I mean, when it's freely available, you know what I mean?
Toni It's very ironic.
Lilly Ennit?
Toni Mm.
Lilly I mean, they're just walking about the streets here. You been outside yet?
Toni No, love; I get all my pleasures indoors.

Lilly You walk hundred yards, guaranteed you get offered heroin, opium, cocaine. It's pathetic—they're doing this to Bryan and people like that just for the publicity. Like they're making out they ain't got no drug problem.

Toni That boy should certainly watch his step.

Lilly Who, Bryan? It's a bit late for that, isn't it?

Toni No, him.

Lilly Oh, him, I couldn't care less about him. I was just making a point, that's all. Here, shall I report him to the Manager?

Toni No.

Lilly I've a good mind to. Maybe I could get him hung as well.

Toni Sleep on it, eh?

Lilly Yeah and all that bollocks she give you: (*she attempts the Lawyer's accent*) "I think Ralph has a better chance of getting off than Bryan..." It's exactly what she said to us. Only with Bryan having a better chance than Ralph! Straight, exactly the same.

Pause. Toni eats a nut

I hope you don't mind—I weren't listening in. I wasn't listening; it's just when I heard her mention Bryan's name. Who'd wanna come here, eh? For pleasure, sort of thing? What is it, part of China really? I meant to get pissed tonight; I hope you don't mind. I open up when I've had a few—as the actress said to the bishop! Cor, I'll give him that, though—he's the first tasty thing I seen since I got here, including the food. Pity he's a pusher. I used to have a boyfriend who was a pusher, bastard. I think that's the worst thing in the world to be, don't you? He's got a nice arse, though, give him that. Have you seen your boy yet?

Toni nods

I'm surprised; they're quite easy-going really, at the prison, I thought. I went to visit someone in Pentonville once. Well, *and* Brixton. They're much worse than here. Makes you think—it would be quite easy to slip him something, I reckon. I could put it in the baby's what's-'is-names. He could sort of hold the baby and gurgle over it an' that and—what d'you think? Think it's worth a try?

Toni Why not?

Lilly It's only fair, ennit? If they're going to have these ridiculous laws. Gives him a chance, dunnit? 'Cos it ain't gonna work, is it, this appeal thing? We all know that, don't we? 'Cept my dad—he seems to think we'll all be going home together and it'll be straight down the pub. But they did hang them Australian boys, didn't they? It's all this national pride shit these foreigners have got, fucking idiots.

Toni The question is—would he have the guts to use it?

Lilly What, the knife? Yeah. He did cut Gary that time. That's my boyfriend—well, ex-boyfriend. He beat me within an inch of my life, so Bryan went round there and give him a stripe.

Toni A what?

Lilly A stripe. (*She gestures a cut down the face*) I dunno what he can do. Sort of get a gun or something… It's only fair he should get a chance, that's what I think.

Toni No, what I meant was…

Lilly Yeah, sorry…

Toni Don't you think he might use it on himself?

Lilly Himself? I hadn't thought of that.

Toni Or, worse still—on the other boy?

Lilly Well, we got to do something, haven't we? We can't just stand by and let a bunch of wogs hang our boys. (*To the Barman*) Yeah, that means you an' all! (*To Toni*) We got to do something, haven't we?

Toni I tell you what—sleep on it. And do something for me, will you?

Lilly What's that?

Toni Call me Toni. Everyone in Marbella calls me Toni. All right?

Lilly Yeah.

Toni That's a good girl. Night night.

Toni gets up and goes

Lilly (*to herself*) Toni. That's a nice name. Used to know someone called that. (*To Barman*) All right?

Lilly and the Barman stand looking at each other as the Lights go down

ACT II

Scene 1

The visiting room at the prison

Bryan is holding the baby, on his side of the desk. Opposite are George, Wendy and Lilly. The Gaoler (and, if possible, other guards) watching closely. There is no visible sign of a knife being passed over, via the baby. Lilly watches but her features are glazed, as ever

Bryan Funny looking thing, isn't he? How's it feel to be on the wrong side of the law, mate? Eh? How's it feel to be a hardened criminal? Yeah? Look, he's smiling, isn't he? Or else he's crapped himself.

George He does smile a lot, don't he, Wend? For his age, like.

Bryan Here, he hasn't *been*, has he? Let's have a look...

George Yeah, they always go on me, Bry—funny that. Only got to pick 'em up and ... whoops. It must be some sort of property I got in my make-up, sort of thing, ennit, Wend?

Wendy It's the only property you have got.

George Yeah, that's true! (*He laughs and coughs*) Cor, yeah, I see what you mean about the upset tummy, Bry. I've had it ever since we arrived, haven't I, Wend?

Wendy Yeah.

George She'll tell you. It's a good thing we got an adjoining toilet 'cos I don't think I'd've made it a couple of times, would I, Wend?

Wendy No.

Bryan You got me all in tears, entcha?

George Got them Lomotil that the doctor give us, but I don't think they do any good really. There's nothing as good as antibodies.

Bryan Whole fucking place is anti-body, ennit?

Lilly You ain't got room in you for no more pills.

George Yeah, that's true! (*He laughs and coughs*) Bleedin' cough...

Bryan Here you are, take him back... (*He passes the baby back to Lilly*)

Lilly All right?

Bryan Very nice.

Pause. No-one knows what to say

So what about this MP of yours, then? What's he gonna do?

George (*beginning*) Well——

Wendy It's too late; it's just the Prime Minister now.

Bryan Yeah. Funny, ennit? I mean, they ought to make drugs legal and put an end to all this once and for all. Then them that wants 'em can have 'em and you don't get pushers and people corrupting minors and mugging little old ladies an' that to support their habit. Stands to reason. When they gonna bring this in? They're thinking about it in America, it's gotta come. Fifty years from now no-one's gonna believe they done this; they're gonna say fuck me, that's completely outrageous, like not letting women have the vote an' that. I mean I'm only twenty, aren't I? Are you sure everyone understands that? I been trying to get that across to 'em but I'm not sure it's what's-'is-name—registered. I'm not sure they registered the fact. Tell them I'm only twenty.

George Yeah, all right, Bry; I'll tell them at the office...

Bryan So what about the Prime Minister, then? She's supposed to be popular with the rest of the world, isn't she? Always poncing off abroad and meeting blacks an' that... Her word's got to mean something, I would've thought.

George Oh, definitely. Say what you like about her, the rest of the world leaders look up to her, don't they, Wend? Apparently she's the only foreign head of state that Americans have heard of, even. I was reading about it in——

Bryan Well, why don't she come out here, then? They're not gonna turn her down to her face, are they? I mean I'd fucking do it. If it was an Englishman being held by foreigners ... 'course I would. Wouldn't matter what he'd done. 'Cos I got pride in my country. It ain't no trouble for her, is it? I mean, the Government pays for her, dunnit?

George Yeah, plus she'd get some free publicity out of it. I'm sure all this has been taken into due consideration, Bry—I mean, we got no idea what's going on behind the scenes, have we, Wend?

Bryan Yeah, well, if only they'd bloody tell us something. Goin' mad in here. Give us a smoke, for Christ's sake.

George gives him a cigarette. His hands are shaking, much worse than Bryan's. In fact Bryan has to take hold of George's in order to get the light. It's a small moment of tenderness which passes quickly

Didn't I need that.

George You are getting enough fags and that, I hope, Bry? Because I did——

Bryan Yeah, yeah, I just left 'em behind, didn't I? Funny, no-one pinches our fags now.

George Yeah? Why's that? Oh—yeah.

Pause

Bryan Dunno what to talk about, do I?
Wendy I'm sorry, I...
Bryan No, no, it's all right.
Wendy What about the other boy? How's he?
Bryan He's all right. Don't show his feelings much.
Wendy His mother's at the same hotel——
Bryan Yeah, well, he's a cunt, isn't he?
Wendy —she's on the same floor.
George (*picking up from Bryan*) Yeah, well, she's an unusual woman.
Lilly What do you mean she's an unusual woman?
George What I say, she's——
Lilly Yeah, well, it don't mean nothing, do it? Unusual woman—what's it mean, she's got two heads or something?
George What I mean——
Lilly You don't know what you fucking mean.
George If you'll just let me finish...
Lilly Oh, you haven't finished yet? I thought you said she was an unusual woman—I thought that was it.
George I was going on to say——
Lilly You're always bleedin' going on...
George May I?
Lilly 'Course.
George Is it all right with you?
Lilly Feel free.
George Thank you.
Lilly It's all right.
George She must have had him very young.
Lilly Not necessarily.
George She can't be more than forty-five, Lil.
Lilly She's forty, she told me.
George Yeah, well, there you are, that's quite young, ennit? Oh, I see what you mean now... Not as young as you, eh?
Lilly (*making a simpering face*) "Not as young as you, eh?"
Bryan Shut up, will you?
Lilly Sorry, Bry, but he's really been winding me up, you know what I mean?
Bryan I'm the one who's fucking wound up, aren't I?
George Yeah, sorry, Bry.
Bryan I mean, you can do all this when you get home, can't you? You can fucking tear each other to bits then.

Lilly Not me, mate; I won't be there.

George Oh, really? You've found yourself a flat, have you?

Lilly Maybe.

George Oh, that's very interesting, Lilly; you must tell me all about that.

By now they realize that Wendy has been driven very low by all this. She isn't actually crying but she's obviously very demoralised

Bryan One thing I won't miss. Oh, yeah, there is something. Listen. About the papers...

George Oh, yeah, we wanted to...

Lilly Shut up...

Bryan Will you listen! About the papers: I don't mind, all right? It just come as a shock when you told me, that's all, but I been thinking about it and I want to say I don't mind. I don't blame you; I'd do the same, wouldn't I? Just make sure you sting 'em for every bastard penny, that's all. Bleedin' vultures.

Wendy I do feel awful about that.

George They caught us on the hop, I suppose it was really. What do they call it? Doorstepping, ennit?

Lilly Shut up...

Bryan You should go back to England. If it happens, it happens, fuck it.

George 'Course, the other thing is the Queen.

Lilly What's she gonna do? Hit 'em with her handbag?

George No, they listen to her, don't they? Because this used to be a colony, didn't it? You know there are some places here, they still believe Queen Victoria's alive.

Lilly Oh, that's useful.

George No, what I'm saying is—there's a lingering affection.

Lilly Lingering affliction.

George I'm just trying to be positive, thank you, Lilly.

Lilly Oh, is that what it is? Thanks for telling me.

George We've just got no idea what's going on.

Lilly That's the truest word you said yet, mate.

Bryan (*to Wendy*) Oi, listen, you know my room? I dunno if it's still my room—what was my room. I got these—I dunno—stories and songs an' that in there, right? Shit like that, done 'em when I was a kid, didn't I? Well, they're in the drawers, right? (*To the others*) You don't have to listen to this. (*To Wendy*) They're in the drawers, in the bedroom; they're hidden in the drawers in all these exercise books, right? They're easy to find; they're just shoved up the back. It's just old bollocks, stories and songs like what every kid writes. Do me a favour, right? Get 'em out and chuck 'em away. And don't read them! I mean it—I'm deadly serious; don't even look at them.

It's the most serious thing I ever asked, right? I really don't want you to even cast your eyes over them. Just chuck 'em straight out. All right?

George (*after a beat*) Yeah, all right, Bry.

Lilly He wasn't talking to you.

Wendy I know.

Bryan Thank you. (*Then*) What d'you mean, you know?

Wendy I've always known they're there.

Bryan What, always?

Wendy Yeah.

Bryan Well, why didn't you say?

Wendy Because they were private to you. Because you hid them.

Bryan You knew they was there, but you never said nothing?

Wendy Well, I knew they were private to you, didn't I?

Bryan Yeah, I know, but—why didn't you tell me?

Wendy Because...

Bryan You read 'em!

Wendy I looked through them.

Bryan You looked through 'em—my private things and you never mentioned it! You must've put 'em back just how you found 'em. I mean, if you'd seen 'em, why didn't you encourage me? Eh? I mean, all I needed was a bit of encouragement, wasn't it?

Lilly Encouragement? You must be joking, mate.

Bryan Don't you understand anything? I could have been something. How d'you know that wasn't a gold-mine in there? I could have been something— a fucking song-writer, or something. Instead of the cunt I am.

George Shh, never mind now.

Bryan I dunno—I just don't get the point, do I? I mean, I obviously just don't sort of—get it. Fucking best thing for me, I reckon. (*To Gaoler*) You reckon that, don't you, Abdul? Win a ticket in a raffle, cunt don't even know what country he's going to! I tell you a secret—I don't even know where I am! They tried to show me on the atlas once; I couldn't be bothered to look. (*He laughs*) Fucking Martian's got more idea than I have. Where am I, d'you know?

George Well, it's Malaysia, Bry.

Bryan Ta, Dad. (*He stands up*) I dunno if this is gonna be the last time or what...

The Gaoler whispers to him

He says I got to say goodbye, just to be on the safe side. Nice way of saying things, haven't they? Not definite, but...

They embrace one by one

(To Lilly) Take care of yourself, girl.

Lilly Might be seeing you, eh?

Bryan I don't think you know what it's like, actually. *(To Wendy)* See you, Mum; just try and forget it, eh? *(To George)* Dad. What a bastard, isn't it?

Bryan goes

George Come on. We'd better go and see if there's any developments.

Wendy Hang on, wait a minute—I never said... He's just gone, hasn't he? I wanted to say something to him.

George Come on.

Lilly lingers

Come on then, Lil.

George exits

Lilly Fucking Pakis.

Lilly goes

The stage is empty

Toni enters

She goes and sits where Wendy had been sitting. She waits

Ralph is brought in by the Gaoler, led in wrist chains

He sits where Bryan had been sitting. He kisses Toni on the cheeks

Ralph Apparently this could be the last time, although stays of execution are sometimes, you know...

Toni It's all happened so fast.

Ralph *(imitating hysterical female)* "It all happened so fast, officer!" I hope your cats are all right.

Toni My cats are all right.

Ralph Pity I never got out to the old hacienda.

Toni It's a pity we—lost contact. I'm sorry, I've not been leading a very reputable life.

Ralph It's all right; this is not your confessional.

Toni No, I just.

Ralph It's not your fault; you're just too young to be a parent, I guess.

Toni (*smiling*) Yes.

Ralph So what you reading at the moment? Always got a book on the go, my old ma.

Toni I only ever read one book, love. *I Ching.*

Ralph Really? What does it say?

Toni I haven't asked it.

Ralph No, good idea.

Toni Let's be businesslike...

Ralph Oh, yes, let's. Sorry, was I getting a bit emotional there? I expect the pressure's getting to me, by God!

Toni I want you to tell them the names you know.

Ralph Ah. Yes, I believe there was something about this in Court.

Toni Tell them the names. That's all they want. I know for a fact.

Ralph You do?

Toni They don't want to do this to you.

Ralph Yes, I've noticed their marked reluctance. Well, they don't have to on my account, you know.

Toni So just tell them the names. It's only one or two they want—the man who supplies in Malaya; they don't care about Australia or America.

Ralph I'm just the small fry, am I?

Toni So you see, there's no point in protecting them, is there? They're not doing anything for you.

Ralph I don't know; they might be tunnelling under here right now.

Toni You only have to——

Ralph You know you're very naïve. They can't go back now. The whole thing's been set in motion. Officials have been assigned; the front page is being held. Sell your story like the other guy's parents...

Toni You know I would do anything for you. Anything.

Ralph OK.

Toni I've even suggested one or two things, but on balance they appeared to be counterproductive...

Ralph What if I gave them the names and they *still* hang me?

Gaoler Ralph, listen to your mother.

Toni That's a risk.

Ralph It is, isn't it? Ah, they want to hang me. They've got the taste. Besides, what about the other kid? I go free and he swings? Even I wouldn't pull a stroke like that. How d'you know I was in here? Get the *Daily Mail* out in Spain, do you?

Toni Just tell them the names. Tell me if you like.

Ralph Tell you? Are you kidding? God knows what you'd do with my contacts.

Toni Tell me the names. Just one name.

Ralph Oh, we're down to one name now. You're compromising already.
Toni Tell me the names.
Ralph That's more like it. Mickey Mouse.
Toni Tell me the names.
Ralph What's in a name? You get the name, but you don't get the person, do you? Not the essential...
Toni You've only got to tell me a name; they'll never know—just tell me the names.
Ralph Blah-blah.
Toni Come on, tell me the names.

Pause

Tell me the names.

Pause

Tell me. Tell me the——
Ralph Oh, stop saying that; it's getting monotonous. And it isn't the point, you know. It really isn't.
Toni Tell me the names.
Ralph Jesus.
Toni (*very calmly*) Tell me a name. Whisper it in my ear.
Ralph We're not allowed to whisper.
Toni Tell me a name and leave the rest to me...
Ralph I don't know any names! OK? They're not that dumb—it's all done through a whole system of middlemen; you don't even get to meet them. I've only met other schmucks like me, and they've passed on. I only let them go on thinking I know names because—who knows? Because I want them to think it, OK? Maybe I wanted them to think I'm somebody. Somebody more than I am. So it isn't the point, see? Am I making myself clear now? I know nothing—there's no way out.
Toni Make up a name. Anyone you half-know, anyone you know. It'll buy you time.
Ralph Anyone I know or half-know? OK, I'll give you a name. You ready? Ralph. How about that. (*He stands up and prepares to go out*)

Toni stands up quickly

Gaoler Ralph! Kiss your mother.
Ralph (*returning*) He's a big family man, you know. These Sikhs are like that; they don't understand us, our—understatement and all that shit. (*He laughs*) Something rather universal, kind of eternal in this scene, don't you think? Mothers and their sons—you can't beat it.

He goes to give her a peck on the cheek but somehow the embrace very quickly becomes impassioned: she covers him with kisses and they hold each other tightly. Toni calls out his name, etc.

Toni (*adding in a final whisper*) I love you, I think the other boy's got a knife!

Ralph is taken away. They separate reluctantly

SCENE 2

The prison cell. It is very hot

Bryan and Ralph are slumped on their separate bunks, with their shirts open. No chains. With them is the Gaoler. He is a bit dozy

Bryan Oi, shit-for-brains, talking fast, all right?
Ralph What?
Bryan Talking *fast*, all right?
Ralph OK.

They speak very fast and colloquially

Bryan I got a blade.
Ralph Yeah, I know.
Bryan How d'you *know*?
Ralph What is it?
Bryan Like a kitchen knife, about six inches, sharp as a bastard.
Ralph (*a little too clearly*) What do you want to do with it?
Bryan Careful!
Ralph All right…
Bryan Dozy bastard… Dunno, do I? Thought you might have some ideas, full of ideas, you are, as a rule.
Ralph We wouldn't get past the door.
Bryan I know we wouldn't.
Ralph Even if we got the gun off him.
Bryan I know.
Ralph You weren't thinking of that, were you?
Bryan I don't know. I ain't completely stupid.
Ralph So what do you want to do with it?
Bryan I'm thinking, aren't I? Fucking do him with it, couldn't I?

The Gaoler looks at Bryan; Bryan smiles at him

All right?

Gaoler What language are you talking?

Bryan It's English, isn't it? You don't know everything, do you?

Gaoler You're crazy, boy.

Bryan (*to Ralph but looking at Gaoler*) Shall I give him a stripe down his face?

Ralph Don't be dumb.

Bryan Got a better idea, have you? Could do, couldn't I? (*To Gaoler*) No, you don't know what we're talking about, do you? Thought you knew English, didn't you? But you don't, do you?

Ralph Shut up.

Bryan I could fucking scalp him like a chicken. I mean—might as well hang me for something I done, didn't they?

Ralph You "done" something.

Bryan Met you, that's what I done.

Ralph Start messing around with these guys, you'll really get it. They'll *hurt* you, d'you understand?

Gaoler No, not so much "hurting"—don't worry.

Bryan Bloody waste, though, isn't it? I mean, maybe we could get as far as the front gates, use the bastard as an 'ostage sort of thing... You'd like to smell the fresh air at least, wouldn't you?

Ralph Yeah.

Bryan I mean I gotta do something with it, haven't I?

Ralph Why?

Bryan What d'you mean, why? You're always asking why all the time. What's the matter with you? When you're dead you won't know the fucking difference.

They both laugh

Ralph You could just as easily have not come by it, you know.

Bryan Yeah, well, I *did* come by it, so shut up. You never, did you? 'Spect you're gonna go along meek as a lamb, aren't you? Yes sir, no sir, shall I put my head in now sir?

Ralph If you're so desperate to do something with it——

Bryan I'm sorry I told you about it now...

Ralph —You could always do me with it. Really, I give you full permission, any time you like.

Bryan Typical. You scumbag; you're always thinking about yourself, entcha?

Gaoler What you are giving "permission" for? What are you talking about?

Bryan Can't you be fucking careful.

Gaoler (*to Bryan*) Hm? What was that? I will bring the chains.

Bryan Nothing, Mr Guard, sir. We was just saying careful or we'll wake up that nice guard of ours.

Gaoler I am not sleeping.

Bryan (*to Ralph again*) No, the only pleasure I got left is seeing you go to that scaffold.

Ralph Yeah, I'd hate to deny you that...

Bryan That's gonna be so nice to see, I'll tell you...

Ralph ...I hate to disappoint you but they put hoods over our heads.

Bryan Yeah? They tell you that? Fucking hell—that's worse than animals, ennit? Even an animal's got more dignity than that. How d'you know that anyway? You always gotta make out you know everything. I suppose you done it before.

Ralph I've seen it in the movies.

Bryan Hilarious. I seen it in the movies. It might be different, it's what I'm saying.

Ralph It's really burning a hole in your pocket. Give it to him.

Gaoler Give what to me?

Bryan Now look what you done.

Gaoler What have you got?

Bryan Satisfied? (*To Gaoler*) I'll give it to you in your Paki guts, pal.

Pause

All right, watch this.

Pause: no-one moves. Then, suddenly, Bryan pulls the knife and holds it in striking distance of the Gaoler

Ralph You idiot.

Bryan You touch that gun, Abdul, I'm gonna rip your fucking guts open, all right?

Gaoler OK.

Bryan All right?

Gaoler OK, I understand.

Bryan I'm glad you understand. You hear that—somebody understands me all of a sudden. I wonder why that is.

Ralph So what's next?

Bryan Don't touch that gun, all right?

Gaoler I am not touching it.

Ralph He's not touching it.

Bryan Whose side are you on?

Ralph I just don't want you to...

Gaoler You know, you will go nowhere with this. It is impossible. They won't let you.

Ralph He knows that.
Bryan Do I? All right, maybe I do. All right, tell you what. Say this after me:
I am a Paki. Go on—"I am a Paki".

The Gaoler speaks calmly, as though humouring a child

Gaoler "I am a Paki."
Bryan I am the lowest form of life.
Gaoler "I am the lowest form of life."
Bryan It's me they should be hanging, not you.
Ralph Shut up.
Gaoler "It's me they should be hanging, not you."
Bryan Bryan.
Gaoler "Bryan."
Bryan Right. You can have it now. (*He gives the Gaoler the knife*)

*The Gaoler takes it. He bears no resentment. Bryan sits down again. He
buries his head in his hands*

I'm dead!

Scene 3

*The final scene is set in George and Wendy's hotel room, leading up to the
time of the executions. However, there are two brief "cutaway" scenes at the
prison*

At the start the room is empty

*After a while, Lilly comes in from her room. She is wearing nothing much and
her hair is tousled. She searches around in a suitcase, finds a carton of
cigarettes and returns to her room, slamming the door*

*Silence until the entrance of Wendy, George and Toni. They look downcast
and exhausted, although Toni retains a sense of defiant jauntiness. She has
a large duty-free bottle of whisky with her. She pours everyone a stiff one and
hands them round. They drink without speaking*

Toni Do you want to put the TV on? I don't know if you'll want it.
Wendy May as well. (*She turns on the TV, switching channels*)

But they all seem to be the same: light music. She leaves it on, with the sound

*down. From time to time they all look in its direction to consult it, but there
is never a news programme. They all sit in silence with their drinks*

Toni Will you excuse me a minute? I'm just going to my room for something.
  (She goes some way, returns, picks up her bag) Tsk! I'd forget me 'ead!

Toni goes out

Silence again

George She's a nice woman really, don't you think? I think she's more upset
  than she looks. I think she probably needs the company, don't you?

Wendy doesn't reply; she drinks her glass dry

Wendy Give us another of that.

George gives her more whisky. He looks at the bottle

George We should've got some of this, but I never saw the place at the airport
  where you're supposed to get it.

*Wendy is drinking fast, like a seasoned drinker. They both light cigarettes.
George stares blankly at the TV screen*

Wendy She in there?
George I dunno. Want me to look?

*Wendy doesn't answer, and he doesn't move. George holds out his shaking
hand*

  Look at that. It's 'cos I'm expecting that phone to ring any minute, isn't it?
Wendy *(with a scoffing laugh)* Are you? I weren't hanging around them
  prison gates just so the bloody telly could film me.
George No.
Wendy I mean, was I?
George No. No way.
Wendy Fuck that. Don't do no good, does it?
George No.
Wendy What have I got to live for?
George Yeah.
Wendy I'm serious. I want to know. What have I got to live for?
George Well, we'll see when we get back, won't we?

Wendy Will we?

George Yeah, well, leave it till then, eh?

Wendy You bring 'em into this world and what do you get? Shat on. That's what I am, every way I turn. Shat on. Give us that bottle. Can see you used to work in a pub, the measures you hand out.

George Don't overdo it, eh?

Wendy Bollocks. You look after yourself.

George No, I'm just saying, aren't I?

Wendy Well, don't say—shut your hole. (*She pours herself another*) Sorry, I know you mean well, don't I? (*She holds out her hand*)

He doesn't quite know what it's for. Then he realizes that she wants him to hold it. He complies. They stay like this for a while; him standing there, and her drinking

Eventually, Toni enters and breaks it up. She is bright-eyed, almost perky—she has taken cocaine

Toni That's better. I left my door open in case the phone, you know.

Wendy That's right, Toni; I was going to say.

Toni You never know; the Queen might have a rush of blood to the head.

Wendy I think they've turned her down.

Toni Fat lot of good's having a queen then, isn't it?

Wendy Sorry, I've had a few.

Toni That's what it's there for; I've got another bottle.

George Yeah, 'cos we couldn't find the duty-free at the...

Toni No, I always pick up a couple of bottles when I'm on the move. I don't suppose you do cocaine, do you?

They look at her. They can't think of anything to say

No, I never used to—but since we went to live in Spain, quite a lot of it seems to pass our way. I find it comes as quite a relief. Mother's little helper.

George Tell you the truth, Toni, we don't really know what it is. I mean, we don't sort of move in that realm, you know what I mean?

Toni No, I just thought I'd offer. Just let me know if you want to do a line. (*Jauntily*) As we say!

Pause. They look at her, wondering about her. She is detached, sniffing

Wendy All I can say is—I hope he had the guts to use that knife, take one of 'em with him. I do, honest. Ah, what am I talking about? Don't pay no attention. What's the time?

George Twenty-to.

They look at the TV

Wendy Television looks worse than ours, if that's possible. What I've seen
   of it. What's it like in Spain?
Toni It's like having a hangover. We get *Dallas* and that sent out on video.
Wendy Do you?
Toni Yeah, daft, isn't it?
George No, not if you want to watch it.
Toni I'm not bothered really. Not real, is it? No-one lives like that.
George No, but I think a little bit of fantasy, it's all right. Harmless, isn't it?

*Pause. Wendy has finished yet another drink. By this time Toni has noticed
her drinking*

Toni I'd take it easy if I were you, love.
Wendy You would, would you?
Toni Yes, I would.
George Yeah, you know, Wend, because.
Wendy (*to Toni*) Well, you're not, are you? You're not me. And you already
   said I was to help meself. This is *my* little helper.
Toni I'm not being mean.
Wendy (*filling her glass again*) That's all right then, isn't it? Cheers, eh?
   Here's to merry old Pe-nang. Arse-hole of the world where only turds can
   live. (*She drinks*) Wallop. Down the hatch. Eh, George? Down the jolly old
   hatch. Yes, mate.

Pause

   Anyway, better than killin' yourself on drugs, ennit?
Toni I don't think there's a...
Wendy No, there *isn't* a lot of difference, is there? Is that what you were
   going to say?
Toni Yeah.
Wendy I thought so. Doctors give you pills, they ought to give you this.
   You've got to go with something, haven't you?
Toni That's right.
Wendy That's right. This is it. Know what I mean?
Toni I thought you might want to keep a clear head because...

During the following, George moves to look through the mini-bar

Wendy What for? What for? What good's a clear head? Tell me—I'm really asking. Who wants to see things clearly? You'd fucking do yourself in, wouldn't you? No, mist it all up, mate. (*To George*) What are you doing?

George We haven't touched nothing in here, Wendy. Here, d'you reckon they keep a check on how much of it you had?

Toni Oh, yes. They do that before you pay your bill.

George Oh.

Wendy I ain't paying my bleedin' bill.

George They got lots of little miniatures and that... What's this? Vodka. Good for your nerves, that. (*He drinks it in one*) All on the *News of the World*, eh, Wendy? What's this? Same again? Don't mind if I do. (*He drinks that too*) Funny drink, vodka. No wonder the Russkies are going to ban it, 'cos it drains the appetite to work. Cuts back the working hours, sort of thing. Just the thing, really, ennit? Let's have a look... Dunno what that is, but it's got to go the way of all the others. (*He drinks another*) Quite a bit in here, Wend, when you look.

Toni You haven't got to drink all that; you've got the Scotch here.

George No, I thought, a bit of variety, you know. Beer, that's boring, ennit? (*He continues knocking back the contents of the mini-bar*)

Wendy I know what I wanted to ask you, Toni. Lilly says you asked if she'd like to go out to Spain, is that right?

Toni Well, I said she could come and stay if she wanted.

Wendy Stay?

Toni Yes, once this is over and done with, if she felt like it.

Wendy Yeah, but not anything longer, like?

Toni Well, we didn't set a time, you know. Whatever holiday she gets.

Wendy Well, her whole life's a holiday—in time, anyway. Not so much otherwise.

Toni Yes well, perhaps we ought to be thinking of the boys now, don't you think?

Wendy Oh, yeah.

There is an uneasy pause

Toni All right, come on; there's no point in dwelling on it.

Wendy It's terrible—I know I should be thinking about him, but—my mind just sort of drifts, you know? It's terrible, isn't it?

Toni It's because you're free, love.

Wendy I don't feel it. No, it's just that she seems to be under the impression that you asked her for something more, you know. I don't know what she thinks, really, but she seemed to have the idea you was after a sort of live-in au pair or governess or something.

Toni Oh.

Wendy I thought it was a bit funny, but I never said nothing.

Toni I don't think I would have said that, Wendy. Because I don't need anything like that.

Wendy No, that's what I thought. She's probably made a mistake about how you live and that.

Toni Yes.

Wendy It's what I thought really, but I never said anything.

Toni I've not got any children or anything.

Wendy No.

Toni Sorry if she's got the wrong idea.

Wendy Well, she... I don't know what she thinks, really.

Toni I expect she's very upset.

Wendy No, I haven't told her yet...

Toni No, I mean about her brother.

Wendy Oh, yes. Yes.

Toni I'll straighten it out with her; don't worry.

Wendy Mm. I ought to warn you—she's had quite a lot of disappointments, one thing and another. You know, she might *react*, sort of thing.

Toni God, it's so easy to raise people's expectations, isn't it?

Wendy This is it.

Toni I just don't need anything like that.

Wendy No, that's what I thought.

Toni I have a woman that comes in and does everything I need. I just meant if she wants a break, you know. She could come out and sit by the pool and all that.

Wendy Yeah, well.

Toni Same goes for you, of course.

Wendy Oh, right, yeah.

Toni I thought it would take her mind off it all.

Wendy Yeah, that's nice of you. Funny how we can sit here, talking like this, isn't it? Nobody would believe it, would they? Expect us to be—I dunno— wailing. (*She drinks*) It's all crap, isn't it? What they say in the papers.

Toni I don't know about you, but I'm glad of the company.

Wendy Yeah. George is all right, but he's not really company, you know.

Toni That lawyer said she'd be with me, but—it's not the same with a foreigner, is it? They don't understand us, no matter how educated they are.

Wendy Well, I'm sorry, I think if I saw that one again I'd definitely kill her.

Toni I think she was just a bit out of her depth really.

Wendy Yeah, well, why did they give her a job like this? I mean, it's too important to entrust to someone like that. They wanted to put a man on it. No-one listens to a woman, and out here I expect it's even worse.

Toni It's hard to take a woman doing that sort of job seriously. I mean, they look daft in the clothes, for a start. I'm sorry, but it's a fact of life. Women should stick to what they know best.

Wendy That's right. God help us!

They both laugh—as best they can. Silence as they look blankly at the TV.
George is still at the mini-bar. He's had to accept the beer. He's pretty drunk
by now

You didn't bring that stuff in with you through the airport, did you, Toni?
Toni What stuff? Oh, the coke. No, love; I've never done that in my life. You
can always score, no matter where you are.
Wendy Good, 'cos I was going to say.
Toni No, that would be the icing on the cake for this lot, wouldn't it? The
mother an' all.
Wendy Yeah, they'd love that.
Toni There's no shortage of offers on the street here.
Wendy Doesn't it hurt your nose? I couldn't bear to put anything up my nose.
Toni I've never thought about it really.
Wendy I'd take heroin, you know.
Toni You *would*, you say?
Wendy Yes, I've often thought about it. I never have taken drugs, but I would
take heroin. I wouldn't want to fart around with pot an' that—I'd go
straight for the hard stuff. (*She stops talking*)

Toni watches her

George Don't seem to be nothing else in here.
Toni Oh, yes, you can soon clear out a mini-bar.
George Reduced to drinking beer, I am.
Toni You can have a go at mine, if you like.
George Can I?
Toni If you want. I'm not touching mine.
George Might take you up on that, Toni.
Wendy If you can stand up.
George 'Course I can stand up... (*He staggers to his feet. But he looks lost*
and groggy. He stares at the TV. Then he picks up the bottle of Scotch. He
looks at it for a second, as though it's an opponent, then he pours it down
his throat. It is a joyless, desperate act)

The women say nothing about it. He puts the bottle down

Long time since I done that. (*He slumps on the bed*)

All of a sudden Lilly barges in from the next room. She is still not fully
dressed and her mascara has run. But she doesn't care

She runs straight to Wendy and throws herself into her arms. It is a shock because she is too big for this sort of thing and also because there is clearly no common warmth of this kind amongst the family as a rule

Wendy Oh, you *are* in there... Oi, mind me cigarette!

Lilly doesn't care about what an intrusion she's being. She sits or kneels still for some time, heaving a succession of sighs. Wendy comforts her, Toni watches

It's all right, Lil, it's all right...
Toni It's all right, pet.
Wendy We're just amongst barbarians, that's all. We have to accept it. There's nothing we can do.

Lilly rises to her feet

Lilly (*finally*) All right, Toni?
Toni As well as can be expected, love.
Lilly What's the matter with him?
Wendy We're all having a drink.

Lilly looks around for a moment. Then she turns and goes quickly back to her room

Toni She's an emotional lass, that one.
Wendy She can be when she wants to be.
Toni She's a real Cancer.
George (*wailing*) I worship the ground she walks on!

The two women look at one another. There is the suggestion of a smile

I'd do anything for that girl. Swing for her, I would.
Wendy Yeah, well, one's enough, ennit? God, the things you find yourself saying. You know what I said yesterday? I said we'll have a proper holiday afterwards, with the money. I was meaning the money we'll get from the papers, you know. It must have sounded awful to her, 'cos she was around, you know—Miss Snooty. But I didn't mean it like that; you just find yourself saying things, don't you?
Toni I know.
George It's all right; it's only family talk.
Wendy Oh, you've revived, have you? Anyway, who cares what she thinks. I doubt whether she's even a proper lawyer. They probably just gave her the case 'cos she's no good. It was all cut and dried, wasn't it? Let's face it—they never had a chance, did they?

Toni I did think I could do something. But we're only human, aren't we?

Wendy Got your return ticket, have you?

Toni Yes.

Wendy That's good 'cos you don't want to hang around here, do you?

Toni I bought one outward and two home. (*She eats a nut*)

Wendy Oh.

Toni So—if you know anyone that wants a one-way to Madrid.

George You can get a refund on it, Toni.

Wendy Tsk, George!

George She can. The hotel'll do it for her.

Toni I'm happy to pay it. Pay it. It'll be the last expense I'll incur in that direction. I'll go home with an empty seat next to me. Can have a good old stretch out.

Wendy It's a fucking farce, ennit? (*She drinks*)

Toni She's got a nice side to her, your daughter.

Wendy Lilly? Oh, yeah. She keeps it hidden, but.

Toni I should have liked a daughter, I think.

Wendy Still not too late, is it?

Toni No, I wouldn't want to go through all that. I mean, someone I could talk to *now*. But then—I don't lead that kind of life really, I suppose.

Wendy Why, what sort of a life you got to lead?

Toni I've not even kept up with Ralph all these years. Because I don't want him to see what I'm doing. Not that I'm doing anything *terrible*, you know—but there's nothing like your own family to make you feel bad about things. No, I don't know how I'd go on with a teenage daughter; I'm probably all right as I am.

Wendy Well, you'll have to settle down, won't you, Toni?

Toni I expect I will, love.

Wendy It comes to us all, you know.

Toni I know, but—I feel all my life as though nothing is real—and I'm sleepwalking through it.

Wendy Yeah, well, it's all those drugs, isn't it? You've got to be more like the rest of us, haven't you? Bored housewives an' that.

Toni I don't like stepfathers for girls. I'm not settled with anyone, really, to tell you the truth. Not in my mind, like.

Wendy You can't have everything, can you? I mean—I wouldn't mind living out in Spain and having a woman to come in and do for me, would I? But there you are: you can't have everything.

Toni I'm not complaining.

Wendy And daughters—I mean, they talk to anyone but their mothers. I'm the last to hear of anything, I am. She defies her parents something awful, that girl.

Toni She thinks the world of you.

Wendy Oh, yeah? She tell you that?

Toni says nothing

Got a funny way of showing it.
George I think the world of that girl.
Wendy Yeah, we know, you'd do anything for her.
George I would.
Wendy Yeah.
George I would.
Wendy All right; we're impressed.
George I know she ain't got nowhere to go 'cos I asked her and I know she'd be telling us left right and centre now if she had. Rubbing it in, she'd be. (*He swings his legs off the bed*) I think I feel a bit better now.
Wendy Why, what have you done?
George What time is it? Oh. (*He lights a cigarette*) I worked in a pub once. I wasn't very old, was I, Wend? 'Cos it was before we was married. Really rough part of King's Cross, it was. Bloke come in one night with a couple of mates. Really big bastard, he was, looked like a boxer or something. He had a wild look in his eye, looking for trouble, sort of thing. I served him. I could hear him saying to his mates: "I feel like I'm gonna kill somebody tonight". And it was like he really meant it, you know? You know when someone really means it. "I'm gonna kill somebody tonight." Anyway, I gave him his change and it was the one and only time in my life I done it, but I short-changed him, didn't I? It was a genuine mistake, like—but I went and short-changed him. God, you should've seen the look on his face when he realized. Like I was a sort of sausage he wanted to chop up. I shall never forget that look. That's how I feel now, ennit? Like some big mean bastard's gonna come and chop me up.
Toni They live very close to the edge, Scorpios. I always count my change. You have to in Spain; they'll try anything. They despise you if you don't.
George (*more to himself*) But I had to pick him, see? Of all the people I might have made a mistake with—it had to be that big mean bastard.
Toni Don't worry about it, George. You can even get to enjoy being a Scorpio.
George Eh, how d'you know I'm a Scorpio!
Toni It's written all over your face.
George Is it? What's she, then?
Toni (*frowning*) I don't know about Wendy. I don't like to make guesses.
Wendy I don't know what I am, so you needn't worry.
George November the 15th—that's when I was born. Is that Scorpio, is it? What, we like to sort of live dangerously, do we?
Wendy He'll probably go off and get a job window-cleaning now.

George (*laughing to himself*) How about that? That's incredible, that is. I'm gonna go and get your mini-bar, if that's all right.

Toni Help yourself, love. Drink the buggers dry, that's what I say.

George staggers out

Wendy You'd think they'd have something on the telly about it, though, wouldn't you? If only out of respect. I can't hardly believe it's happening.

Toni I'd be very worried about you, Wendy.

Wendy What? What d'you say?

Toni I said I'd be very worried about you.

Wendy You *would* be? How's that, then? Sorry, I'm not with you.

Toni Perhaps it would be better if I said I *am* worried about you.

Wendy What, just 'cos I said that about heroin? It was nothing—I think it's normal to want to try everything. See what all the fuss is about. Or you think I'm an alcoholic—is that it? Well, it's not a big deal, is it? I mean, how many alcos are there? Bet you're a bit of one. You can shift it; I seen you. Can you guess that sort of thing, or did I tell you? 'Cos I'm not a *bad* one; just an everyday one, you know what I mean? I just like a tipple every day; who doesn't if they're honest with theirselves? I did try to give it up once, mind, but I couldn't. Couldn't give it up. It hurt, trying. So I stopped trying and now I don't mind it. You live with it, don't you? You feel something coming on—you fight it or you—step inside of it. I sort of stepped inside of it and started living with it. It's not a big deal, is it? You can see that in my face, can you? I thought you was trying to sort of sus me out; I caught you looking at me a couple of times. It's all right; I don't mind. I'll tell you something, though, seriously. It isn't such a bad thing to be. It's the one thing in life you can sort of rely on. What I think is—so long as you're honest with yourself you're all right. Long as you don't tell yourself lies. I mean, what's wrong with getting pissed? I'm not rolling around on the floor, you know. You'd hardly notice it. What I say is—all these things, they been put on earth for us to enjoy, so why not enjoy 'em? It's just killjoys with problems of their own want to stop you. That's what I think it is. We'd be all right if it weren't for people like that telling us how to behave. They wanna look after theirselves, instead of. Fucking television, look at it. It's twenty-four hours now, isn't it? Must think we can't do without it. Must think we're all... They say it insults the intelligence—you heard 'em saying that? Makes me laugh, that does, 'cos if they asked me I'd tell 'em I *like* having my intelligence insulted. Why shouldn't it be? *I'm* insulted, aren't I? Every day. Do you know what I do for a living, Toni? Did I tell you? Bet you can't read this in my face or whatever it is. I go to a canteen in Malet Street; I stand there in this stupid turban-thing and I say "Custard or cream? Custard or cream...?" (*She repeats it a number of* *times*) You've no idea what a twat I feel. I mean, I'm only waiting for the day I'm replaced by a fucking parrot. But there you are. The question has to be asked, doesn't it? Otherwise, how's anyone gonna know whether they can have it, custard or cream? They can have a choice, you see? That's very important for people, that is. If some twat don't ask the question—well, I mean, it's complete and utter chaos, ennit? The whole system breaks down. You can say something now.

Toni They should have self-service.

Wendy Ah, but I wouldn't have the job then, would I? Then we'd both be out of work, me *and* him. See, that remark, it's typical of someone that don't know. "They should have self-service." Maybe they ought, *but what about me*? I mean, up the workers and all that. That's typical, that is. I mean, why not everything machines? Do without us altogether. Why not? I don't need to stand there like a twat, do I? They ought to pay me for stopping indoors, didn't they?

Toni People have to work somewhere.

Wendy Exactly, they do, don't they? Bastards have to if they want their little luxuries. Soft toilet paper, a little day out. A tree at Christmas, a bit of 'olly on it. This is the first holiday I've had in ten years—do you believe that?

Toni I think people complain too much in England.

Wendy Cor, you're probably gonna say Mrs Thatcher's doing a good job in a minute.

Toni I don't like her as a person but I do admire her.

Wendy Yeah, me an' all. She sorts 'em out, don't she? I voted for her, didn't I? George never, but I did. Fuck all she's done for us, though.

Toni I think she's probably tried her best.

Wendy Anyway, you're quite right—I *do* complain. What's more, I ain't gonna stop. Anyway, what do you do that's so clever, you haven't got to slave away like the rest of us?

Toni Don't worry, love, I work.

Wendy What at then?

Toni I married a crook, love.

Wendy Well, that ain't work, marrying somebody.

Toni All right.

Wendy I mean, is it? Any prat could do that. I think I did actually, but look where it's got me.

Toni I don't work in a canteen, I grant you that.

Wendy No, I was just saying.

Toni It's the only way you can get anything these days, and hold on to it. There's no money in being honest.

Wendy Sorry, but I find that attitude's exactly what's wrong with England today.

Toni Do you?

Wendy No.

They both laugh

Toni Everyone says they miss it, England. The green fields and the brown
cows and the sausages and the football and the autumn. Not me, I don't
miss a damn thing. Never look back, me.
Wendy I never look forward. What's there to look forward to?
Toni Don't ask me.
Wendy Oh, I thought you was a sort of an agony aunt, like they have in the
TV Times.
Toni No.
Wendy Oh, I must have been misinformed.
Toni The only thing I do know is—you've got to take risks. Calculated risks.
Wendy God, that's all I need, ennit?
Toni Anyway, Wendy, this is hardly the day to go into our...
Wendy IT NEVER IS THE DAY! Sorry, it's 'cos I've had a few. Usually
I can hold it. Straight, I can drink a bottle of that stuff and you wouldn't
know it. That boy of yours killed my Bryan. Bryan took a risk, didn't he?
He could easily have given that ticket to someone else, said it was too much
for him, but he didn't—he took a risk and it killed him. I could kill you. I
might yet. 'Cos you're a pusher, just like him. That girl's not going within
an inch of your place. Cocaine, and your boy's about to be hanged for
drugs! Excuse me, but I think that's very sick. Fuck this big mouth of mine.
But I mean it. Well—no, I don't mean it. I'm sorry, I don't know what I
do mean. I don't know.

Toni puts her arms round her. Silence

*The Lights go down on the hotel room. Another part of the stage: The prison
cell*

*Ralph and Bryan, chained and dressed for execution. With them, the
Gaoler and (if possible) various other officials*

Gaoler All right, Bryan, is there anything I can do for you before you go off?

Bryan shakes his head

Ralph? Is there anything I...?
Ralph (*suddenly*) No! No, nothing. Yes! I'd like to see Paris before I die. (*He
laughs*) No-one gets it! It's a *line*, man. It's a line from a W.C. Fields movie.
W.C. Fields—great movie star. No-one knows! I'm dying amongst fools.

Gaoler Just wait a...

But Ralph is starting to have a fit. He goes berserk. The Gaoler grabs the chain and dodges around with Ralph. Ralph is not trying to hit anyone; he is like a crazy man having a fit. He can't control any of his movements, or his voice. He cries out "No, no, no!" etc. All this time, Bryan watches, completely still and silently aghast. He smokes his cigarette. It goes on for some time. Ralph is eventually restrained—or the fit burns itself out. He gets to his feet. No-one speaks for a while. Ralph continues to shake. The Gaoler appears to be awaiting a signal from somewhere

Ralph (*inaudibly*) How's the cigarette?
Bryan What?
Ralph How's the cigarette?
Bryan It's all right.
Ralph Is it?
Bryan Yeah.
Ralph Shouldn't smoke, get cancer. Call that gallows humour, you heard of that? You know what I'm talking about?

Bryan says nothing

I can't free my hands. I'm never gonna see my hands again. Jesus, I love my body. Love every inch of it. My lovely, precious body.

Pause

Bryan Oi. Here's another fine mess you've gotten me into.

They both laugh

Gaoler OK, boys. Say goodbye, please.
Ralph Goodbye.
Bryan 'Bye.

They go to each other and embrace as best they can. Bryan is very still. The scene ends

Lights up again on the hotel room. Toni still has her arms around Wendy. They separate

George enters. He staggers in, carrying Toni's mini-bar. He puts it on top of his own

Wendy You didn't have to bring the whole thing in.

George I want to see what's in it, don't I?

Wendy Well, you could've done that in there.

George Yeah, well, you know...

Wendy Oh, please yourself, you want to give yourself a hernia, that's your look-out.

George Let's see... Eh, they've given her lots more than they give us.

Toni They must have been anticipating my requirements.

Wendy God, I ought to be there! What am I doing? Don't you think? I mean, just because I didn't want to be photographed, that ain't a reason, is it?

Toni You wouldn't do any good, love.

Wendy No, but at least I'd be there, wouldn't I? God, that's me, that is. Always in the wrong place.

Toni That's why they hang men. Because it upsets the women. Don't give them the satisfaction.

George You wouldn't want them all staring at you on the telly, would you?

Wendy Yeah, but it's my boy, ennit? Comes to something when you can't put yourself out a bit. I mean, I ain't gonna do anything for him again, am I? Couldn't I get one of them rickshaw-things? They understand English, don't they? (*She waits for them to answer, but they don't. Besides, she doesn't make any move and soon seems to forget her suggestion*)

George Gin, that must be.

Wendy What you drinking that stuff for?

George It's the mini-bar, Wendy.

Wendy I know what it is; I'm saying—it's *theirs*, ennit? What you drinking their liquor for when we got our own? (*To Toni*) He can't hold his drink, see.

Toni Let's kill the bottle, shall we?

Wendy Thought I already had.

They drink

Toni Queen's messenger on his white horse is what we want now.

Wendy Useless fucking Queen. Probably sitting under a pile of dogs, and them stupid sons of hers. God, don't you hate 'em all?

Toni (*unsure*) Well...

George The Royal children, you know, they're brought up with special trousers—they got no pockets in 'em. It's so they can't put their hands in their pockets. Did you know that?

Wendy What you drinking?

George Dunno, haven't got me glasses!

They both laugh and cough

Wendy He always says that: what you drinking? Dunno, ain't got me glasses.

George It's especially poignant in my case 'cos it's true.

Wendy Get him—"poignant". What's that mean?

George Means poignant, dunnit?

Wendy Yeah, I know, but what's it *mean*?

George Means what it sounds like.

Wendy Sounds like you're pissed, mate.

George That's true.

Wendy You're pissed, amigo. Isn't the, Toni? I suppose some people live like this all the time, don't they? I don't think you can make money if you're honest. That's what I think. What do you think?

Toni Mm.

Wendy I don't think you can. Government's got it all worked out, haven't they? You make a square bob and—wallop; they're on to you. What's your racket, darlin'?

Toni Oh, I don't know.

Wendy Oh, yeah, you married well, didn't you? That's it? See, you didn't ought to say things like that; you didn't ought to put yourself down.

Toni I haven't got a racket of my own, love.

Wendy Yeah, but you're not short of a bob or two, are you?

Toni I manage.

Wendy Yeah, you're a glamorous woman. Ain't she, George?

George What's that?

Wendy I'm saying Toni here—she's a glamorous woman?

Toni Shut up, love, for God's sake.

Wendy Yeah, all right.

Toni Don't take your frustrations out on me. You've got a lot of good qualities—use them and stop complaining. I've never heard anyone complain so much as the English.

Wendy Maybe we got a lot to complain about.

Toni But you've not been anywhere. Have you? You've not seen anywhere else, to compare yourself with.

Wendy Bryan went somewhere, didn't he? Look what happened to him. (*Suddenly to George*) For God's sake, will you stop drinking them fucking things! (*She snatches one of the bottles from him and hurls it across the room*) I keep hearing this bloody unscrewing sound; it's driving me fucking mad. If you're gonna drink, drink like a man.

George Right. (*He stands up, but almost immediately sinks down again*) Oh, dear...

Wendy Christ—it's not funny, is it? (*To Toni*) Do you find this amusing at all?

Toni No.

Wendy Neither do I. How did we get started? I didn't even notice it starting. What time is it? What are we doing here?

Toni We're taking our minds off it.

Wendy Yeah. Some joke, ennit?

George I'm gonna kill someone tonight.

Lilly bursts in again. She still isn't fully dressed. In her forearm, a needle is sticking out

Lilly (*to George*) Gonna kill someone, are you? That's nice. How about me? (*She moves downstage holding out her arm, for everyone to see*) Here you are. This is my poison—what's yours? (*She sniffs the glass*) Hm, whisky. Didn't know I was on this, did you? Been on it for a year now.

Toni (*quietly*) God, get that needle out of her arm.

Wendy I ain't touching it. Oh Christ.

Lilly laughs. Toni goes to take out the needle

It's all right; I can manage. (*She withdraws the needle, rubs her arm then flings the needle across the room*)

George staggers to his feet

It's good stuff they got out here; I can recommend it.

George reaches her and raises a fist. She doesn't flinch. But the punch never comes. He falls first or else it's a completely innocuous punch. She laughs

Actually, I *did* know you were on it...

Lilly Bollocks, you never...

Wendy ...But I didn't say anything.

Lilly You always got to know everything, you have, haven't you?

Wendy But I don't see why you've got to shock us with it.

George I didn't know.

Wendy I suppose you want to get us all in there with Bryan, do you? Eh? Trying to get us all busted?

Lilly She knows all the phrases, don't she? "Busted".

Wendy slaps her round the face, hard

That hurt.

Wendy Where do you get this from?

Lilly What difference does it make?

Wendy Do you know?
Toni I've got an idea. It wasn't from me, if that's what you're thinking.
Wendy And you want a daughter? Christ, have this one—she's been nothing but heartache to me.
Lilly Gary got me on it; he was a pusher, wasn't he?
Wendy Charming boy. Puts her in the hospital and gets her on H. She'd be better off where you live, amongst the crooks.
Lilly What difference does it make? (*She switches channels on the radio*) Any music on this?
George I'm not in the mood for music, Lil.

She carries on. The music obscures some of Toni's remarks on the phone

Toni (*on the phone*) Hallo, Room Service. Can you send up the barman please? ... To Room 433. I want the barman from the International Bar. ... Yes, if that's his name. Straight away.
Wendy You're not sharing them needles, I hope. You hear me?
Lilly Yeah, I heard. I don't share nothing. It's the way I was brought up. Anyway, I got lots of needles.
George I'm gonna fucking kill this—bottle. (*He drinks lustily. Afterwards he is almost paralytic*)
Wendy I suppose you think you're clever?
Lilly You didn't half hurt me then.
Wendy You think it's shocking or something.
Lilly Well, I'll tell you—you should of seen the look on your face.
Wendy You slut.
Lilly Takes one to know one, dunnit? All right, Toni? All set to go, I am! Viva España, eh? It's all right, I'm not usually like this. I can behave myself usually, can't I, Mummy dear?
Wendy Where is it?
Lilly Where's what?
Wendy This stuff—where is it?
Lilly Why—who's coming?
Wendy I want to try it.
Lilly You? (*She laughs*)
Wendy What's so funny?
Lilly You wanna try it?
Wendy Yeah, me.
Lilly (*to Toni*) What's she on about?
Toni It's nothing to do with me, love.
Wendy (*moving to Lilly's room*) Where is it...?
Lilly Eh, hang on... You haven't got no idea!

Wendy goes into the next room, followed by Lilly

Lilly has found music on the TV. It remains on—not loud as yet. It is crude Malaysian rock. Toni sits still with her drink. George is lying on the floor, or the bed

After a while, a knock on the door and the Barman comes in. He is in his off-duty clothes, dressed like a young stud

Toni Yes, come in, please. Well, you've been putting yourself about, haven't you?

Barman Huh?

Toni Did you sell that young lady some smack?

Barman I don't know what you're talking about.

Pause. They look at each other. He turns to go; she stops him. He reacts—he doesn't like being touched

OK, what d'you want—go to your room?

Toni No, thank you. It's a charming offer, mind.

Barman Room Service said you wanted me, so I don't know. I don't sell no smack. We can talk it over in your room—OK.

Toni Real little animal, aren't you? I think my husband could use a man like you.

Lilly comes in again

Lilly Here he is—Fu Man Chu. Hi, man! (*She smiles and mimes injecting a needle into her arm*)

Barman I don't know what she's talking about.

Toni It's all right; we're not going to report you. Did you think we were going to report you? No, we've asked you to come and dance for us. Haven't we, Lilly?

Lilly Have we? Yeah.

Toni He's going to give us a dance, 'cos we're on holiday.

Lilly He's got a lot of different talents, hasn't he?

Toni Yes, I bet he's a lovely mover. I bet he's got pictures of John Travolta on his wall.

Lilly Yeah, look at all his gold—you could melt him down and make a bob or two, couldn't you?

Toni Yeah.

The Barman makes an ambiguous gesture to Toni—it could be a pass. Toni suddenly slaps him fiercely. He reacts, but checks himself. Toni laughs at him. Even Lilly is surprised

Fancy yourself, don't you?

Barman I gotta go.

Toni No, you haven't. You stop here, love. You're in demand. You go back and you won't have a job to go to. Straight into prison, savvy? No, you're going to give Lilly and me a little dance.

Barman I go to gaol, you go to gaol too.

Toni It's all right by me. (*She smiles sweetly at him*)

Barman You're crazy, you know that?

Toni That's me, love, crazy lady. Turn the music up, Lilly.

Barman OK, who gives a fuck?

Lilly Oh, that's something else he promised to do for me an' all.

Toni Yes, I thought so.

Lilly Fair dos, he's not bad, is he?

Toni Come on—let's see you move it.

The Barman starts to dance, watched by Toni and Lilly. He gets into it. He's good and he knows it

Wendy comes in again. She is grasping her arm. Blood is running down it, from the vein

She stands there, rocking on her feet. At one point, Lilly springs up and plants a huge kiss on the Barman's lips. Then she goes and sits and watches him again. The music continues; the Barman dances. At the end, they are in the following positions, perhaps frozen: Toni is sitting on the bed, looking right through the Barman, and beyond. George is grappling like a drowning man at Wendy. He succeeds in pulling her down. They collapse together. Lilly, unable to control herself any more, makes a rush at the Barman and plunges her hand inside his trousers. She throws her head back in silent laughter. The Barman raises his arms

The Lawyer enters. She appears to have something to say, but she is stopped in her tracks by the scene in front of her

A split-second after the Lawyer's entrance, two hooded bodies are hanged. The sound of their fall echoes

Lights out quickly

FURNITURE AND PROPERTY LIST

Further dressing may be added at the director's discretion

ACT I

Scene 1

On stage: PRISON CELL:
2 bunk beds
Table
2 chairs

Personal: **Ralph:** Sony Walkman

Scene 2

On stage: HOTEL ROOM:
TV
TV remote
Mini-bar
Phone

Off stage: Very small baby (**Lilly**)
Suitcase containing pills and swimming costume (**George**)

Personal: **Wendy:** cigarettes, lighter
George: cigarettes, lighter
Lawyer: business card

Scene 3

On stage: PRISON CELL
Chess
Marijuana joint

Personal: **Ralph:** Sony Walkman

Scene 4

On stage: PRISON VISITING ROOM:
             Desk
             4 chairs
             Lilly's baby

Personal: **Bryan:** wrist chains

Scene 5

On stage: PRISON CELL
             Boxing magazines

Personal: **Ralph:** wrist chains (optional)

Scene 6

On stage: TONI'S ROOM:
             Barman's clothes incl. bow-tie and white jacket
             Tray. *On it*: some drinks
             Toni's pants

Personal: **Toni:** wrist-watch

Scene 7

On stage: HOTEL BAR:
             Ethnic knickknacks
             Well-stocked bar
             Knife
             Lemons
             Cloth
             Tables
             Chair
             Stools
             Nuts
             Glass of beer

Personal: **Lilly:** lighter, cigarettes
             Toni: jewellery
             Toni: lighter, cigarettes, tiny handkerchief

ACT II

Scene 1

On stage: PRISON VISITING ROOM
               Lilly's baby

Personal: **George:** lighter, cigarettes
               Ralph: wrist chains

Scene 2

On stage: PRISON CELL

Personal: **Bryan:** knife

Scene 3

On stage: HOTEL ROOM
               Suitcase containing carton of cigarettes
               Beer

Off stage: Large duty-free bottle of whisky, bag (**Toni**)
               Toni's mini-bar (**George**)

Personal: **George**: lighter, cigarettes
               Wendy: lighter, cigarettes
               Ralph: chains
               Bryan: chains
               Bryan: cigarette
               Lilly: needle
               Wendy: blood

LIGHTING PLOT

Property fittings required: nil. Practical fittings required: TV set
5 interior settings

ACT I, SCENE 1

To open: Bright, hot lighting

No cues

ACT I, SCENE 2

To open: Overall general lighting

No cues

ACT I, SCENE 3

To open: Bright, hot lighting

No cues

ACT I, SCENE 4

To open: Overall general lighting

No cues

ACT I, SCENE 5

To open: Bright, hot lighting

No cues

ACT I, SCENE 6

To open: Early evening lighting

No cues

ACT I, SCENE 7

To open: Overall general lighting

Cue 1   **Lilly** and **Barman** stand looking at each other   (Page 38)
               Fade lights down

ACT II, SCENE 1

To open: Overall general lighting

No cues

ACT II, SCENE 2

To open: Bright, hot lighting

No cues

ACT II, SCENE 3

To open: Overall general lighting

Cue 2   **Wendy** turns on TV, switching channels   (Page 50)
               TV effect

Cue 3   **Toni** puts her arms round **Wendy**   (Page 62)
               Fade lights on hotel room, bring lights up on prison cell

Cue 4   **Bryan** and **Ralph** embrace   (Page 63)
               Fade lights on prison cell, bring lights up on hotel room

Cue 5   Sound of bodies' fall echoes   (Page 69)
               Black-out

EFFECTS PLOT

ACT I

ACT II

Lightning Source UK Ltd.
Milton Keynes UK
UKOW06f0326071115

262204UK00010B/117/P